Crying in the Bathroom

Crying in the Bathroom

A MEMOIR

ERIKA L. SÁNCHEZ

VIKING

VIKING
An imprint of Penguin Random House LLC
penguinrandomhouse.com

LIBRARY OF CONGRESS CATALOGING-IN-PUBLICATION DATA
Names: Sánchez, Erika L., author. Title: Crying in the
bathroom : a memoir / Erika L. Sánchez.
Other titles: Crying in the bathroom (Compilation)
Description: New York : Viking, [2022] |
Includes bibliographical references. |
Identifiers: LCCN 2021054801 (print) |
LCCN 2021054802 (ebook) | ISBN 9780593296936 (hardcover) |
ISBN 9780593296943 (ebook)
Subjects: LCSH: Sánchez, Erika L. |
Mexican American women authors—21st century—Biography. |
Authors, American—21st century—Biography. |
LCGFT: Autobiographies. | Essays.
Classification: LCC PS3619.A517 Z46 2022 (print) |
LCC PS3619.A517 (ebook) |
DDC 818/.603 [B]—dc23/eng/20220208
LC record available at https://lccn.loc.gov/2021054801
LC ebook record available at https://lccn.loc.gov/2021054802

Printed in the United States of America
1st Printing

Designed by Amanda Dewey

For my grandmother Clara
and all the women who came before

A Wounded Deer—leaps highest.

—*Emily Dickinson*

CONTENTS

INTRODUCTION

I grew up thinking I didn't matter, that no one cared what I had to say. The world didn't see me, a daughter of working-class Mexican immigrants, and what it did see, it considered disposable, inconsequential. I rarely found portrayals of anyone like me— bookish and poor and surly and Brown—in the art that I enjoyed. I searched everywhere for a model for the life I wanted, but found few. I wanted to be a writer and travel around the world, but I had no idea how I was going to make that happen. I saw only snippets of that kind of life here and there. Texts like the poetry of Sandra Cisneros were a lifeline. Here was a Mexican girl from Chicago who'd become a writer and traveled alone through Europe. But texts like hers were rare finds for me, because, it seemed, I was the only one in my immediate vicinity looking for them. My teachers didn't often teach books by people of color, and I didn't have mentors or access to the internet, which was rudimentary at that time. The libraries in my community were so limited and hostile toward children that I began stealing books from the bookstore. Today, of course, I know that there were other books out there at the time that spoke to who I was, but they didn't make it into my hands very often. So when no template existed, I did what Lucille Clifton wrote about in her poem "won't you celebrate with me" and made it up.

When I began writing about this life that I'd made up, I was plagued by a nagging voice that asked, "Erika, who the fuck cares?" The answer was always a memory of how deeply affirming it was for me to discover myself in the little art that declared a story like mine worthy. I wanted a place for myself in this tradition, and when I began seeking more texts of women writers while in college, I started to see where I fit in. I consider Toni Morrison the patron saint of my writing. To write with her level of honesty and clarity is my North Star. Virginia Woolf is referenced in this book again and again, both for her work and for her tragic life, which, I suppose, are one and the same. Sor Juana Inés de la Cruz became a model for my rebellion. And the list goes on and on. None of my books could have been written without these extraordinary authors. I'm indebted to all the women who came before, those who paved the way as well as those whose talents were extinguished, buried, or sublimated because the world was afraid of their strength. It's thanks to their rebellions, big and small, that I get to lead this extraordinary life—that is, a life completely of my choosing. I am myself in a world that pressures me to be otherwise, a world that doesn't love me, wasn't built for me.

Women of color are regularly praised for our resilience, but what's too often overlooked is that our resilience is a response to so many forms of violence. For us, resilience is more than a noble trait; it's a lifestyle that oppression has demanded of us. Either we adapt or we die.

Even so, we need not be mere caricatures. Our stories matter, despite what the rest of society would like us to believe. So here I present to you a series of my musings, misfortunes, triumphs, disappointments, delights, and resurrections. I have pieced this all together to the best of my ability, but I also acknowledge that memory is tricky, slippery, alive, and ever changing as the years pass. We all see different versions of the same thing. I have written the truest book I was capable of creating. It's the way I've always made sense of the world and my life. Thank you for being on this earth with me.

THE YEAR MY
VAGINA BROKE

O n a crisp fall day during my senior year of college, I called a local feminist clinic in a state of panic and described, in great detail, what was happening to my vagina. I was standing outside one of my classes, hoping no one would hear me chronicle the goings-on of my nether regions. Weeks prior I had begun experiencing an itching and burning sensation, and I very quickly concluded that I had an STD. The woman on the line was patiently reassuring me that it was likely a "garden variety" vaginal infection, but I wasn't convinced. To me, "garden variety" made it sound like what was happening between my legs was fecund and beautiful, when it was most definitely not. "Are you sure?" I asked, pacing, autumn leaves crunching under my feet. "What if it's an STD?"

Just the thought of it filled me with shame and disgust. It didn't matter that I had had sex with only one person, who was a virgin, with a condom, in the past few months. I was convinced I was a diseased degenerate. Even though I considered myself a feminist, and it was 2005, and I knew that sex—even the casual kind—was not inherently evil or immoral, I believed that God or the Universe or perhaps my pious female ancestors from the great beyond were punishing me for putting out. *Cochina*, I thought to myself.

For the first three years of college, I commuted to campus on the train from my parents' house. It was not at all what I wanted, but I couldn't afford to live in student housing or rent an apartment, not even the dankest of hovels. I hatched all sorts of plans and schemes to gain my independence, but the meager wages I was making from my part-time job at the university registrar weren't enough to keep me from being broke, so I was stuck living with my parents. And they weren't exactly raking it in as factory workers, so there was no possible way I could ask them for money to move out of their perfectly good house. That was some white people shit.

I'd just spent the summer leading up to my senior year studying abroad in the city of Oaxaca (on a big, fat student loan), so living at home for my last year of college began to feel absurd. I had wandered across Mexico alone, nursing a broken heart after my boyfriend of two years told me he didn't love me anymore and quickly replaced me with a homely white girl. For weeks, I partied with the rich Mexican friends I'd met while sobbing on the beach one afternoon. I drank so much mezcal that I gave myself pancreatitis and had to be hospitalized. I had *lived*. Now I'd suddenly be informing my parents of my whereabouts? And at twenty-one? Naw.

So early in the year, I packed my things and moved in with a friend who lived in an apartment across the street from our old high school, about a mile away. My parents were livid. Old-school Mexicans, they considered my leaving home simply because I felt like doing so a violation of my role as daughter. In their eyes, I was both ungrateful and disrespectful, which wasn't entirely untrue, but not because I was moving out. Leaving home at this age, and unmarried, was not something that any women in my family had ever done. It was a stunning and unprecedented affront. But that didn't stop me.

I paid two hundred dollars a month to rent my friend's spare bedroom, and that was half the rent. Her father owned the building, which, I imagine, is why it was so unbelievably cheap. That and the fact that the place was, unfortunately, a dump, with yellowed walls and faded linoleum floors in the kitchen.

I had outrun the roaches of my childhood only to be greeted by them once again—*It's nice to see you, Erika. We missed you.* The kitchen had a clinical yet sordid quality that suggested pain and desperation. Everyone looked sad and gaunt under its fluorescent light. A friend described it as "a place where people would shoot up heroin or some shit." My bedroom wasn't much of an improvement. For some mysterious reason, there was a giant broken mirror resting against one of the walls, and I never bothered to remove it despite the obvious danger. I just used it to look at the lower half of my outfits and pretended the sharp edges couldn't possibly hurt me.

I was so broke that I slept on an air mattress for the first two months. Some nights, I'd wake up flopping all over the place when it had deflated. Needless to say, I slept like absolute shit, and I would have continued to do so if one of my aunts hadn't bequeathed me her old bed. My books, my most prized possessions, were stacked on industrial shelves that were likely purloined from a factory. And I didn't have a closet, so the clothes that didn't fit in my dresser (did I even have a dresser?) were strewn all over the place. When it was hot, I writhed in bed all night without an air conditioner; in the winter, I wore layers of clothes to keep from shivering. Another friend visiting me one evening took one look around and said, in disbelief, "Wow, you live like Charlie from *Willy Wonka and the Chocolate Factory*." I was mildly insulted, but proud nonetheless to be living on my own with no one else's help.

With such limited income, I learned to strategize about food. My friend and I ate lots of pancakes, eggs, and pasta that year. It was then that I understood the food of my childhood: flautas de papa, sopa de fideo, Mexican spaghetti, refried beans. Starches and fats were the cheapest way to get full (duh), but it had never occurred to me until I bought my own groceries. I also drank many five-dollar bottles of wine because it made me feel so adult to buy them at the grocery store. All those years anxiously waiting to drink legally and the time had finally come. Look at me being a lady of the highest sophistication.

I AFFECTIONATELY CALLED this my "slut year." (Little did I know, there would be other iterations in my future.) Despite not actually having much sex, I dated frequently to get over my breakup. Rather than pausing to assess my own wants and needs, I distracted myself with men. I went out with men I wasn't even attracted to, partly out of boredom, partly out of a desire to be desired. Friends of friends, guys at bars, classmates, whatever. I was an equal opportunity ho.

Not surprisingly, some of the fellas were tough on the nervous system. There were times I was certain I wouldn't be interested in a second date but agreed to a first just for the hell of it. I couldn't stand to be alone with my thoughts. I made a lot of bad choices at this time. For a brief spell, I fucked a virgin who once answered his mother's phone call while he was still inside me. I just stared at him, mouth agape, while he argued with his mom in Polish.

Like most college kids in their senior year, I was eager to attend any party or alcoholic gathering I was invited to. No time was too late for me to leave the house; no night was off-limits. I could be coaxed out of my apartment, and out of my pajamas, at ten o'clock on a night before an exam. I would change quickly and run out of the apartment to meet friends at whatever gross dive bar was hopping at that time. It was almost always a guaranteed disappointment, but I went because *what if it turned out to be the best night of my entire sad life?*

Several weeks into the school year, my friend Martha had an early Halloween party in her small attic apartment. She lived in the neighborhood on the South Side called Back of the Yards. Martha was a few years older, and I had known her since high school. We'd been in college together for a while, but by my senior year, she had dropped out. I had always looked up to Martha, because she dressed Goth and liked to talk about books. She introduced me to new authors, clove cigarettes, and a lot of new wave and alternative rock bands. She had vague aspirations of becoming a writer, but follow-through was not her strong suit. Also, her butt sloped inward, which I feel factors in somehow. You be the judge.

There was always something insidious about Martha—a back-handed compliment, a critique cloaked as tough love, a harsh observation about my appearance. Bad vibes, spirits, energies, jujus, and vapors galore. Martha would always hurt my feelings, and because I wanted her approval, I would brush it off and convince myself that I was too sensitive, which is what everyone in my life had always insisted. My sensitivity had always felt like a curse I needed to break.

During Martha's party, a man with a beautiful brown face began flirting with me. He had also gone to our high school and was a few years older. His name was José. My memory of José was hazy. All I could recall was that he'd gotten his high school girlfriend pregnant their senior year. He was attractive in an obvious sort of way, so I didn't consider him a romantic option at first—I preferred a more understated handsomeness, a face with character. He knew he was hot, too, and looked like he was perpetually posing for a photo, lips pouty and eyes feigning deep thoughts. I always believed that these kinds of men weren't interested in me, as I considered myself an all-around weirdo. I kept looking about to see if maybe I misunderstood and he was actually speaking to someone else, that perhaps there was another, hot girl behind me. But no, it was me he was eyeballing. I shrugged it off and walked around the party with a giant goblet of wine that seemed to refill itself. At one point, I was so drunk I had to lie down on my friend's bed. A few minutes later José came in and closed the door.

It was the drunkest I had ever been, and I could hardly hold myself up. José and I made out for a while until I had to push him aside to throw up. Most of it landed on the bed. At some point he left and I fell asleep in my own vomit.

The next morning I found Martha and her boyfriend at their kitchen table drinking coffee. My head throbbed and my stomach was sore from throwing up, which had been not only poorly timed but also violent. To this day, I've never been more hungover than I was that morning. I felt like an old mop that had been wrung out. I apologized to Martha and her boyfriend for ruining their sheets and promised I would replace them. They assured me that it was fine, that sometimes shit happens.

"How did it go with José?" Martha smiled coyly. She wasn't wearing her signature black lipstick and her face looked both blank and unsettling, like a fraught canvas.

Something tugged deep within me, but I couldn't name it at the time. Part of me felt like maybe she had done me a favor, since, you know, he was so hot and all and I was such a weirdo.

"We made out, then I threw up, so nothing happened," I said. Maybe I even laughed.

"He was looking for you, so I told him to look in my room. You're welcome," she laughed.

I used to believe that rapes happened in dark alleys and parking garages. I thought they had to be physically violent, the man forcing your legs open. I was a child of the '90s weaned on after-school specials and made-for-TV movies about innocent white girls losing their virtue at the hands of a psychopath. It was all "No means no!" I had never considered that rape could happen when you're so drunk you can't even hold your body upright and you're vaguely attracted to the guy who creeps into the room where you're fading in and out of consciousness. We didn't talk about consent, let alone ongoing consent, enthusiastic consent. We didn't talk about slut-shaming, toxic masculinity, and misogyny in women, about the interconnectedness of all these things. We can't identify what we don't have the language for. And so I didn't have words for what had happened to me. I knew that whatever it was, it felt wrong, but I wasn't entirely aware of why I felt that way.

Martha's behavior left me uncomfortable, like I was wearing an itchy shirt that I just learned to ignore. It would take me a long time to understand the gravity of what she had done—many years after, we stopped speaking. I'd asked her for a safe space to lie down, and she'd offered me up for the taking. We fought a lot that year about things unrelated to what had happened at her party. It was as if my mere existence offended her. After one such fight, another friend of mine began referring to her as "Selena's killer." He'd seen a picture of the two of us at a party where I am smiling at the camera while she is scowling and looking at me sideways. She legit looks like she is about to murder me. Martha and I eventually had a giant falling-out, which seems to have been inevitable, as she turned out to be a hater in the highest degree. We made a few feeble attempts to reconnect over the years, but I stopped after she randomly went nuts on a benign Facebook post of mine.

MY VAGINA CONTINUED to itch and hurt, and I couldn't stop thinking about it. The situation seemed hopeless until I had my first appointment at the Chicago Women's Clinic. I had volunteered there a number of times, and so I knew and respected their philosophy and had a lot of faith in them as a result. The practitioners, most of whom were nurses and midwives, didn't cover the lower half of your body during exams, because they believed it was important that you see and understand what they were doing. They also warmed their speculum (as everyone should), and the stirrups were covered with knitted cozies. The clinic had been around since the 1970s and the outdated wood paneling made me feel like I was sitting in someone's grandma's house in rural Wisconsin.

During my initial visit, a nurse offered to show me my cervix in a mirror. I was nervous and even skeptical for a moment because I had never seen it before—I was only familiar with my outer layers—but I agreed. I knew I shouldn't be afraid of my own body. I was a feminist, after all.

"See, it's pink and healthy," she said, smiling. Despite the infection, my vagina appeared to be in good shape.

"Cool," I said too eagerly. "Wow!"

The truth is that I was startled. I wanted to feel empowered, but it was like looking into a wet alien maw.

There I learned that the drama was just a yeast infection. That was my first diagnosis. I don't remember what they prescribed that time. This seemed like a simple problem with a straightforward solution; that is, until it refused to go away. For the first time in my life, I became well acquainted with my vulva. I studied it closely in a hand mirror every day, hoping it would go back to normal, but, having never looked before, I wasn't even sure what normal was. My vagina was a mystery to me; it was high time to take a good look, I thought. *So many folds.*

For months after the initial diagnosis, I tried every possible medication and remedy to make the itching and discharge go away—over-the-counter ointments, oral prescriptions, and probiotics that I both swallowed and inserted inside my vagina. I even put raw garlic cloves inside me a few times, but all that did was make me smell like garlic. Not a delicious situation. I upped the ante and made multiple appointments with my primary care doctor, but she was clueless. She just kept prescribing the same medication over and over again. I would have sold my soul to Satan for a new cooter, I told my friends. Was it possible to get a vagina transplant? Was the science there yet?

When I lost all hope in my primary doctor, I made many more appointments at the Chicago Women's Clinic. They prescribed me an oral antifungal, and I held my breath as I filled the prescription, as though it contained not only medicine but all my hopes and dreams.

I DATED JOSÉ—and I use the term *dated* loosely—off and on for months. All the while, I was so terrified of getting an STD that I never had sex with him, even when my vagina was healthy and eager. I was attracted to him and I truly wanted to be fancy-free, but my persistent vaginal challenges put me into a never-ending state of anxiety. The thought of anything else going wrong in my crotch made me clam up, you feel me? We'd be kissing and groping and whenever I reached the precipice, I would yank back my desire and leave his place with a throbbing between my legs.

My whole life I'd been taught that giving in to temptation would make me cheap and common, like the girls I had been warned about—the girls with the heavy eyeliner and the dark lipstick who ended up pregnant before graduation. In theory, I so wanted to be sexually free, to be in charge of my own body, to be a woman who gave the finger to tradition and gender norms, but I didn't yet understand the complicated tapestry of sex and shame for a Latina, and for me specifically. On the one hand, you grow up with beautiful women on Spanish-language TV proudly shaking their chichis, and on the other, you have your mom talking shit if you dare shave your legs before your fifteenth birthday. It's confusing.

So José and I went through this back-and-forth routine several times until he tired of me and broke off whatever the hell we were doing on Valentine's Day. Dude lived in his mom's basement and had two baby mommas, and this rejection *still* hurt.

The summer after college, José died in Lake Michigan. I heard that he had been swimming with his friends and he never surfaced. I suspected that he was both drunk and high at the time, since I had never seen him sober. I think my last words to him were "Fuck you."

I went to the wake by myself and sat in the back, because how could I explain who I was? The girl who wouldn't put out, here to pay my respects.

MEN CAME AND WENT, but the infection persisted. It was tenacious; it had moxie; it had gumption. An axe to grind. It would disappear and then come back with a vengeance. I continued going to the Chicago Women's Clinic every several weeks, and they gave me all sorts of different treatments. During one visit, they allowed me to look at my vaginal culture under the microscope. The slide was filled with mauve shapes that resembled branches. It was almost beautiful, like an abstract painting of a meadow. I was finally face-to-face with my enemy. *You motherfucker*, I muttered silently.

During another visit, my cervix was coated with gentian violet, and for days afterward, every time I peed, it would trickle out and make the toilet water turn a beautiful shade of purple. To my disappointment, the only thing that did was stain my underwear and make my trips to the bathroom more memorable.

After months of failed remedies and medications, I cut sugar and carbs from my diet. It was a painful choice for me then, because it meant I couldn't drink alcohol, which was the only way I knew how to socialize. During nights out with friends, I drank to smother the depression and anxiety that was always lurking in the bushes of my mind. I drank until I literally couldn't think, until my body felt soft and warm and free and everything was funny until it wasn't. I wanted so much to slosh around in a temporary oblivion. But the cost of it all was waking up with a brain encased in spikes and an existential despair that left me practically comatose as I watched reruns of *Sex and the City* for hours on end.

The pancreatitis I got after my study abroad in Mexico that previous summer was a result of this behavior. Of course, I vehemently denied that there was any connection at the time. When the doctor treating me at the hospital pressed me about my drinking habits, I acted offended. What did my aching pancreas have to do with the mezcal I guzzled every night? How dare you, medical expert!

Apart from cramping my style, the no-carbs life was also expensive. All at once, I was trading in pasta and pancakes for vegetables and protein, and I was hopeless at preparing either of those things for myself. Sometimes I'd go to a salad bar during my lunch break and hold my breath at the register as they weighed my bowl.

Occasionally, the infection would subside for a while and I'd be so elated that I almost wanted to throw a dinner party to celebrate its departure. When it inevitably returned, thoughts of it were all-consuming. Like any misguided stupid-head with internet access, I kept googling the causes of persistent yeast infections and eventually learned that the two most common causes were diabetes and HIV. I knew for a fact that I didn't have diabetes, so I convinced myself that although I had always used condoms and was not in a high-risk population, I had HIV and was going to die of AIDS, to my family's utter shame. This kind of catastrophic thinking was a regular by-product of my tendency to spin ridiculous, elaborate, and, in this case, woefully ignorant tales and believe them wholeheartedly. The first time I ever masturbated, I was certain that God had seen me and that I would burn in the pits of hell. When I started actually hooking up, I thought I might be pregnant after essentially dry-humping an acquaintance of mine. Though there was no penetration, I convinced myself that there was a fetus growing inside me, and that my life was over thanks to the abortion restrictions for minors in my state. Needless to say, the sex education I received was abysmal, full of shame and fear tactics. All of us were expected to abstain from sex, which made the day-care for the children of students in our school more than a little ironic. I don't remember learning much about birth control. Most of my knowledge came from the radio show *Loveline*, which I listened to in secret every Sunday night. The shitty sex ed combined with my wild imagination and paranoia was enough to make me believe that sex was going to kill me.

FALL TURNED TO WINTER and then spring, a time when Chicagoans begin to reemerge from their caves wizened but hopeful. It was then that I mustered the courage to get an HIV test at the Chicago Women's Clinic. I was already there to get my vagina checked out again, so I figured I might as well. Afterward, I took a walk in the neighborhood, soaking in the sunshine and blooming flowers and trees. *Everything is going to be OK*, I assured myself.

But OK was a far and distant land, one I barely knew. This was before the rapid finger-prick tests available now, so I had to wait an entire week before returning to the clinic for the results. I don't remember much about that week apart from how endless it felt as I obsessively imagined a positive result. I knew that if I had HIV, I would not be brave. I would not be one of those people who use their personal tragedy to empower others. I would collapse in a mire of self-pity and misery. I was no hero.

The morning of my appointment, I drove with my friend Lawrence, who I had accompanied months before to receive his own test results. I remember walking up the stairs holding his hand. I was shaking and my legs felt like they would fold under me.

"Oh my God," I said over and over again.

Dorothy, one of my favorite clinicians there, was in charge of giving me the results. She had a wry sense of humor and a raspy voice both from years of smoking and from what I imagined to be some hard living.

"Negative," she said and smiled, exposing her long, stained teeth.

My heart leapt. "Thank you so much," I said as I hugged her tightly. I don't know how common hugs are in a medical setting, but she kindly hugged me back.

DRIVING HOME AFTER a date that spring, I took the expressway in the wrong direction. I've always been ditsy like that, my head forever in the clouds. I was so out of the way that I ended up on the opposite side of town near a North Side bar where my friends had told me they'd be drinking. I hadn't planned on going, but since I was already in the area, I decided to stop by. A tall, attractive man named Sam was with the group. He seemed halfway intelligent, so I offered to give him a ride home at the end of the night. Instead, we wound up in my apartment making out and groping each other. My vagina was unimpaired at the time, and though I wanted very much to have sex, I was so frightened that I stopped myself from going any further. In my imagination, Sam and I would date, and I would eventually give it up after a respectable amount of time.

He didn't pay for my coffee the next morning, even after I drove his ass home, way across the city—didn't even offer. Also, he was a mansplainer, tried to tell me what an ionic column was. Bitch, please. I took art history, too. He was two things I still can't stand in a man: cheap and condescending. Still, we continued to see each other.

The consummation of our flimsy courtship weeks later was . . . anticlimactic. I was finally giving in to my urges after battling a yeast infection that had lasted from the fall through the winter and continued making cameos in the much warmer months. (Can you believe that shit? We almost had an anniversary.) So much inner turmoil had given way to my eager and throbbing vagina, and in the end, I was disappointed beyond my wildest imagination. Sam, having little to do with the desire that consumed me, was also no match for it. For my ferocious appetite, he offered only scraps. The sex was sad not simply because Sam's penis was incredibly small, but because he had no idea what to do with his hands, mouth, or incredibly small penis. He was neither generous nor attentive, either ignorant or indifferent to the function of the clitoris. I scowled and rolled my eyes as he penetrated me from the back. I felt absolutely nothing.

IT WAS A wild and impulsive year, and it was a studious year. I was lucky to have had a case of very level-headed senioritis. I often studied and went to class when I was sleep-deprived or so hungover I felt like a flaccid party balloon. (A slutty nerd? A responsible thot?)

I've always wanted the impossible in my life, my dreams downright unreasonable. My future was uncertain, but I knew that I would travel and write no matter what. I applied for a Fulbright in Spain and three MFA programs in creative writing, and I began an application with the Peace Corps. That spring I was also inducted into Phi Beta Kappa and received the undergraduate poetry award.

I was in the Honors College and was set to graduate magna cum laude. I didn't know what would happen, but I felt unstoppable.

I held on to my part-time job at the insurance brokerage for most of my senior year. Because I lived like a fucking pauper, my paltry earnings were enough for me to survive on my own. As I sat at my desk one afternoon, I received an email informing me that I had received the Fulbright. I couldn't breathe, though I wanted to scream. I stared at the screen in disbelief. I, Erika L. Sánchez, was going to live in *Madrid*.

All at once, it seemed that everything everywhere was full of promise, even between my legs. Sometime in late spring I found the magical cure for my never-ending infection: tea tree oil. After I followed some instructions I found online for a douche using the oil, my poor frazzled vajayjay finally recuperated. I was desperate and had tried everything, even things I hadn't run by my doctor or clinician. It was a shot in the dark, and somehow it worked. Sure, I'd gone totally rogue, but I had run out of options. I had been ready to turn to astrology, for Christ's sake. Maybe the stars knew something I didn't.

I felt like a new person, no longer disgusted by or frightened of my body. I lived with a newfound exuberance—the world was beautiful and anything was possible! Sometimes I wanted to stretch my arms out and frolic in the streets like a fool.

But then the discomfort returned a few weeks later. My vulva felt so raw that at times it hurt to sit down. I wondered what I had done to deserve this. Why couldn't my elbow hurt instead or some shit? What kind of karmic retribution was this? Why did God hate me so? I went back to my primary care doctor to see if she could solve this new mystery. Why would I be in so much pain if my infection was gone? I had lost most of my faith in her, but I didn't know how to find another doctor through my parents' insurance. And I feared exposing myself if I searched too hard.

The nurse that day was cute in a bland white-guy kind of way, and I was embarrassed to talk to him about my aching pudendum. I was relieved when he exited the room. My doctor examined me and said she suspected herpes. I gasped. I'd never even considered that a possibility. How could it be? I hated her at that moment—her blond hair, her sharp features, the judgmental look in her eyes. I began to sob on the examining table. She had no idea what to say to me, so she scurried out of the room and sent the nurse back in to draw my blood.

My car's air-conditioning wasn't working that day, so I drove home crying and sweating in the unbearable Chicago heat. Then I felt my tire go flat in the middle of a busy street, and that's when I really lost it. My face was streaked with sweat, snot, and tears. I pulled over and continued to sob into my hands as I baked inside the car. It was all but confirmed: I was filthy.

Those of us who grow up with a vagina must endure all the verbal abuse hurled at our bodies. In Spanish, some of the terms for vagina include: "la cochinada" and "la vergüenza," literally "the trash" and "the shame." We learn that our most intimate parts are inherently unclean, that they are sites of sin and degradation. And when we begin to bleed, we are made to believe that our bodies are expelling a repulsive debris, and we must experience this in complete silence so we don't upset the penis-havers of the world. The first time I got my period, I was so confused that I looked at the brown stains on my underwear and thought I had somehow shit my pants. I never expected my menstrual blood to be such a dark color. Even when I figured out that it was blood, I was so embarrassed that I didn't want to tell my mother. Once I finally did, she gave me a winged pad the size of a small airplane and I sat in my bedroom for hours feeling humiliated.

MY DOCTOR WAS wrong about the herpes. I returned to the Chicago Women's Clinic once more, and this time Dorothy diagnosed me with vulvar vestibulitis, a form of vulvodynia, which is basically chronic vulvar pain with no identifiable cause.

"But why does it hurt?" I asked. "Is it another infection?"

"No. See, there are these spots that are sensitive. That's what's causing the burning sensation."

I winced as Dorothy touched them softly with a Q-tip to demonstrate. Something was wrong with my nerves.

I asked about treatment options and she informed me that vulvodynia was understudied and there were no guaranteed cures. She sighed and gave me a strained smile. I knew she was sorry she couldn't help me. Dorothy and I had developed a close relationship by now. She had become the person most familiar with my vagina. I had a lot of affection for her; she was like an auntie who always kept it 100.

Not knowing what the hell to do with me anymore, Dorothy, that kind soul, referred me to a free acupuncture clinic. There, a woman stuck me with needles that sent little shocks throughout my body. She prescribed Chinese herbal concoctions that tasted so bitter that I shuddered as I gulped them down. But that didn't work either.

I remember when I first learned about the origins of hysteria, or the "wandering womb," according to the ancient Greeks. I laughed as I imagined my uterus floating inside me like some sort of wraith. My experience fit into this archaic tradition. Women's pain has always been oversimplified and disregarded. What is not understood is conveniently assigned to the ethereal.

No one knew what to do with me that year. My pain was a ghost.

ONE DAY IN EARLY JUNE, I walked across the stage in a cap and gown and the four years behind me seemed to evaporate. I was several weeks from my departure to Spain and ready as ever to live. On a night out, I was dancing by myself at a reggae club, all loose and sweaty in a cheap pink tank top and a faded denim skirt. I was a little high from weed I'd smoked with a handsome dreadlocked fellow in the back of the bar who did not return my flirtations. Defeated, I drank a beer and danced with my eyes closed until a dark stranger began dancing next to me.

I kept scanning the smoky room full of damp bodies, looking for the friend who'd accompanied me that night, but she was nowhere to be found. I continued dancing and ignored the man. At the end of the night, he asked for my number, and that's when I noticed he was handsome—his skin was a deep reddish brown, almost copper, his eyes wavered between green and hazel, and his cheekbones were ridiculous. But I was leaving for Madrid at the end of the summer and I wasn't interested in starting a romantic relationship. He pulled out a phone so clunky and old that I was embarrassed for him. It looked like some '90s relic that was held together with tape. I've never been materialistic, but how could I take him seriously? So I gave him the wrong number. But then he accidentally erased it and asked for it again.

ABDUL WAS AN IMMIGRANT from Pakistan and ten years my senior. As a purportedly practicing Muslim, he was scandalized by my lifestyle, even though we had both been drunk when we met at the bar. I'd point out this irony countless times in the future, and he'd find as many ways to justify his behavior. He was a man, after all.

I didn't want to like him—I hated how he judged me, couldn't stand his backward views on gender—but over the course of several weeks, I fell in love with him (or became obsessed with him?) with a desperation that was totally unfamiliar. It swallowed me in its greedy mouth. I had never desired anyone so stupidly in my life and it terrified me. It reminded me of a character from the novel *One Hundred Years of Solitude*, who was so savagely in love that she ate dirt. That's how bad it was.

The pain in my vulva had subsided for the most part, so we spent the summer fighting and fucking. It didn't take me an entire summer, however, to suspect that something was wrong. No, my first clues came within a few weeks of meeting him. Every time I asked to see his apartment, he would have some excuse about his roommate or renovations. Any idiot could have figured it out right away, but my mind wasn't right—I'd get short of breath just look-ing at him.

One night I kept prying, insisting I see his apartment, and Ab-dul finally confessed: he was married. Of course he was. This should have been obvious to me from the start, but the orgasms had clouded my common sense.

According to Abdul, he'd married a Pakistani American woman he'd known for a green card. It was supposed to be a transactional arrangement, but he had inadvertently knocked her up. His son was three and his wife had schizophrenia, so he was afraid to leave her. I would never find out how much of this was true.

His revelation enveloped me in a cocktail of rage and sorrow. Here he was, judging me for being a wanton woman, all while beg-ging me not to go to Spain, and the motherfucker was married. All I remember about that night is that I cried so much that it felt like an aerobic exercise.

When I told a few of my friends the truth about Abdul the fol-lowing day, they were horrified. I was, too, of course. Still, I wasn't ready to leave him. My mind just couldn't adjust to the new reality, or that I stayed with him knowing the truth. What kind of person willingly becomes a mistress? What kind of shameful shit was I doing? Who had I become?

"He doesn't really love you," a friend told me, and I wanted to believe her. I agreed that the entire situation was toxic, but I also felt defensive, because how would she know that? I was dying in-side. All I wanted was for him to leave his wife and be with me. I thought of the short story "What We Talk About When We Talk About Love," by Raymond Carver. In it, one of the characters insists that her abusive relationship with her ex-boyfriend is a form of love. Though he drags her by the ankles and tries to kill her, she is firm in her belief. I always sympathized with her perspective because at that time I was convinced that I loved this man. I didn't consider that our age difference put him at an advantage, or that his desire to dictate aspects of my life was a thing that some might have called abuse. To me, we were star-crossed lovers in a novel. We were epic. We were tragic.

The first time Abdul told me he loved me was after one of our many fights. It started at a downtown nightclub. He had commented on a woman's (meager) ass to provoke me, and it worked. I exploded. I demanded that he take me back home and screamed at him as he drove down the expressway. We fought outside my apartment.

At one point I turned away exasperated. I couldn't believe that I was having such a stupid argument.

"I love you, you know that?" he said.

I did not tell him I loved him back.

ABDUL BOTH ADORED me and treated me like absolute shit. I think we were both addicted to each other. He would tell me he never wanted to see me again and then turn around and make grand proclamations of his love, accompanied by beautiful gifts. The most memorable was a bright orange-and-magenta salwar kameez I'd wear to my goodbye dinner at the end of the summer. We broke up countless times, but one of us would always cave, and we'd end up having earth-shattering sex. Once, we did it on the floor of his friend's empty apartment building—another post-fight coital brought on by an argument that I can't even remember. I can recall only the rain, and that "Come Undone" by Duran Duran was playing on the radio.

IT WASN'T LONG before the pain returned. In the middle of the summer, I was so tired of my aching vulva that I drove myself to the ER at the Cook County public hospital and sat with the saddest-looking people in all of Chicago. I waited to be seen for hours and hours. I did not want my parents to receive a hospital bill for an ER visit, so I opted for free care. I was not about to explain to them that my vagina was broken.

I was usually opposed to male gynecologists, but I was in so much pain that night that when one actually entered my room, I didn't care. *Just please fix me*, I thought. The doctor, a friendly Black man in his thirties, made small talk as he examined me. I told him I had just graduated and when he asked what my plans were, I told him about the Fulbright and my plans to spend the upcoming year in Madrid. The doctor was so impressed, he went over to his colleagues and told them my good news. "This young lady just won a Fulbright!" he exclaimed. "Can you believe that?" It was an odd moment, getting congratulated on my academic achievements as my legs were in stirrups.

I just smiled politely and hoped that whatever he prescribed was going to cure me.

It didn't.

The next day I called in sick to work and Abdul brought me a pizza on his lunch break. I sat on the couch eating with my legs spread open. Sometimes he was so kind and gentle that I almost forgave him for the rest.

I left for Spain in the beginning of September. Abdul hurried me that morning as I ran around my disheveled room in such a frenzy that I knocked over an old beer bottle from God knows when. While I longed for change and wanted nothing more than to see the world and to write, I was terrified. I said goodbye to my first apartment with an ache in my throat. It was dank and sad, but I couldn't believe that I would never live there again.

Abdul and I would eventually end. It was a truth I knew in my spine; I wasn't that naive. But first, he would visit me in Spain and we would have sex as if we were both going to die. We would ride a bus in Granada at sunset. I would sit on his lap, look at the sky, and feel almost desecrated by happiness.

FOR SEVEN YEARS, the pain came in and out of my life. It followed me into my late twenties. There were times I could hardly sit, times I cried in frustration. I added more doctors to the rotation, until one finally recommended something totally novel: physical therapy. I thought she was out of her damn mind. How could therapy possibly cure the searing pain in my vulva? "Are you sure?" I asked her. "That makes no sense to me." I shook my head and stared at her quizzically.

After years of trial and error, I couldn't imagine anything working, let alone something so unusual. I agreed to physical therapy but was armed with my signature cynicism. I was ready to be disappointed once again. During my first appointment, I lay on the table with my legs slightly spread as Whitney, my physical therapist, began to gently stretch my tense vaginal muscles with her fingers. I was startled to feel an almost pleasurable ache, not in a sexual sense, but the kind you might experience when a massage therapist breaks up an impossible knot in your back.

Whitney explained that my body had learned to store stress in my vagina, of all places. Scared Pussy Syndrome, as I like to call it. My vagina was traumatized; she had seen some things. Over the course of several weeks, Whitney showed me exercises to loosen my legs, hips, and pelvis. The tension had migrated to other parts of my body and had become a persistent network. Once a week I held my breath as each of her stretches hurt yet released what felt like lifetimes of strain. Both the anguish and skepticism finally began to unravel. Though there was nothing wrong, my vagina would brace itself for suffering. I had to teach it not to.

DOWN TO CLOWN

I upset white people with my laughter. A friend once described my laugh as a birdcall. One calls it the "señora cackle." Another says it sounds like a Mexican grito, which is probably why it startles the whites. *Oh no, a Mexican is among us!* I definitely laugh in Spanish and I can't deny that it's piercing. A few years ago while I was in a restaurant in Belize with a friend, two white families were visibly unnerved by my laughter, so I laughed harder and clapped like a seal.

A coworker once insisted that my laugh made me sound like a rich lady, as if I were mocking hungry children in ragged clothing and fingerless gloves. It can be heard from long distances, and friends can tell I'm at a party without having seen me. More than once I've received the ire of fellow attendees at movies or shows, and I've just plain scared the shit out of plenty of people sitting next to me. In one such instance, I was sitting next to an insufferable bro in a backward hat at an improv show. He gave me such hateful looks throughout the performance that we got into a spat and I almost punched him in the face. Yeah, I was yukking it up, but it was a motherfucking comedy show, not *Schindler's List*. What was I supposed to do? But that's the thing about laughter, right? When it's genuine, it's something you can't control. I don't necessarily like my voice either. When I sing, it's an unlikely combination of Kermit the Frog and Whoopi Goldberg, a trait I inherited from my mother (*Thanks, Mom*), but I have no choice in the matter. It's the cross that I must bear.

MEXICANS JOKE AS IF it's our moral obligation. I think this is what happens when you're accustomed to hardships. We cope using humor so we don't lose our shit. To me, the most oppressed people, without question, are always the funniest. I don't have any empirical evidence to prove this claim, but it's true. "Poor people laugh harder than rich people," Chris Rock once said in an interview. "Especially black people, they laugh with their feet, too."

Mexicans also laugh with their bodies. If you're not familiar with my people, you'd likely be startled by the boisterousness of our gatherings. We put our entire selves into it. When my family gets together, it's a raucous, sweaty affair. Sometimes I laugh so hard I can hardly breathe. I cry and clap. I shake my head in disbelief and kick my feet. When I was eight, I literally peed my pants after one of my uncles cracked a joke about who knows what, I wish I remembered. I zipped out of the living room and into the bathroom, but it was too late. Everyone knew what I had done, and my uncle henceforth referred to the incident as "the Big One," an allusion to the hypothetical earthquake on the San Andreas Fault. This too made me laugh.

THERE'S NOTHING TO romanticize about poverty, but when you're poor, there isn't much of a compulsion to put on airs. In Mexican culture, we talk freely about poverty in ways that aren't merely clinical. Art that centers on being poor is commonplace. Class divisions in Mexico are stark, much more pronounced than they are in the United States. What's similar, however, is that the few at the top are traditionally white or close to it, while the rest of the country, the darker ones, toil to simply survive. As a people, we have to find humor and meaning in the face of oppression so as not to be defeated by it.

Take the beloved comedy show *Chespirito*, which features a character named El Chavo del Ocho, a boy played by a middle-aged man, who literally lives in a barrel and whose only goal in life is to eat a ham sandwich. A sandwich! Also, consider the stand-up of George Lopez, which mostly explores his impoverished childhood. The first time I heard his comedy I was tickled by his bit about weenies on a fork, because I, too, ate weenies on a fork!

Then, of course, there is Cantínflas, arguably the most beloved Mexican comedic character of all time: a fast-talking working-class fellow who's simply trying to survive in the world. His interactions with the rich are especially hilarious and adept at illuminating how absurd and out of touch they can often be. One of my favorite childhood memories is watching a scene of Cantínflas on the beach massaging ketchup on the back of an unsuspecting wealthy white woman, who of course assumes it's suntan lotion. Que pendeja.

Better to laugh at the absurdity of your time on earth than to resign yourself to mourning all of life's misfortunes. Laughter is a beautiful form of resilience, one that evinces a generosity of spirit. But sometimes I do wonder: Is it brave to find joy amid despair, or is it simply part of being human? Does it even matter?

Throughout my life I've noticed that people with the least tend to give the most. A trip to just about any developing country proves as much. The hospitality of the people in these locales is stunning. I understand that it makes me sound paternalistic, even tone-deaf, romanticizing the proletariat, but it's been my experience. Don't get me wrong, no one deserves to be poor; it's an embarrassment to humanity. But the fact of the matter is that need often fosters both creativity and generosity. It's part of survival. You create a network with the little you have.

I once traveled with my boyfriend—who became my husband, who became my ex-husband—to the mountains of Nicaragua, where we were generously fed by poor farmers. When two scrawny chicken legs accompanied the traditional breakfast of rice and beans, we more than suspected that the family had killed the chicken for us that morning, and at great cost to themselves.

Having experienced this sort of generosity when visiting my own family in Mexico, I was certain this was the case. My family, who subsists on a humble menudo business and the help from those living in the States, will feed anyone who is hungry. My grandmother once took in a family member's child despite struggling to feed her own children.

There's a brutal honesty in our humor that makes me thankful to have been born Mexican. As I was growing up, my family, nearly all factory workers, always referred to work as "la chinga," which literally means "the fuck." What is more honest than that?

So much of Mexican humor is based on what appears to be cruel observations about a person's physical appearance. It may seem rude to outsiders, but to me it shows that we don't pretend things don't exist. We don't have the patience for pussyfooting. A Mexican family will talk shit to your face, while a white family is more likely to wait for you to leave, at least from what I've observed. Personally, I like to know where I stand instead of having someone talk shit behind my back. (Say it to my face, Susan.) If you're bald as fuck, for instance, Mexicans will one hundred percent call you "pelón." I legit thought that was my uncle's name for a long time. Being bald is a fact that we openly acknowledge, and oftentimes, the term is used affectionately. One of the many times I visited Mexico, I met a boy nicknamed Mal Hecho, which literally means "badly made." He didn't seem at all fazed by the epithet, though. He was a portly little fellow with a bowl cut who took it all in stride. On another visit I learned about a man in town called Gorduras ("Fats." Plural!) I was certain that this dude was a good sport about it, too. I'm sure they've had those nicknames since they were kids, and they were probably two of the most beloved characters in town.

On a trip to Mexico a few years ago, my aunt was telling me a story about a woman called La Culpa. "Why do they call her La Culpa, Tía?" I asked. "Porque nadie se la quiere echar," she explained. I almost spit out my drink. The wordplay was remarkable.

Callous, I assure you it is not. It's simply the Mexican sensibility. (I don't know if rich Mexicans operate like this, because upper-class Mexican culture is as foreign to me as Tajikistan.)

I suspect that white feminists would be outraged by this kind of teasing, finding it damaging to a girl's body image, causing eating disorders and such. I know that experiences vary and that the jokes can enter mean-spirited territories, but part of me appreciates that I grew up this way. It may seem counterintuitive, but such ruthless joking about looks actually deemphasized their importance in a healthy way. I learned to develop a thick skin about my own and others' appearances, because it really wasn't that serious. I also cultivated an acerbic wit as a by-product of having to dish the insults right back. And most important, I acquired the skill of poking fun at myself, not out of self-loathing, but as a way of coping with the ache of being a person. What fucked me up the most wasn't the jokes about how gigantic my mouth was, it was the emaciated white women on TV touted as the epitome of beauty, and my grandma calling me fat when I was eleven, because I loved me some Mr. Submarine, and boy did it show. . . . And then the diet my mother put me on as a result of the Mr. Submarine sandwiches.

I'VE BECOME SOMETHING of a student of humor, and of the handful of books that I've read on the topic, one in particular has insights that feel true to what I've always observed. The book is called *The Humor Code*. In it, authors Peter McGraw and Joel Warner seek the human formula for humor. What makes something funny is something I've wondered about for a long time.

Why do we live in a world where people who enjoy Carrot Top, for instance, walk freely among us? Is there a common denominator for humor across cultures? Are dick jokes universal?

The book argues that comedians are similar to anthropologists in that they have the ability to see beyond themselves and empathize with people who are different, which is why, the authors maintain, "ethnic and cultural outsiders in America" have succeeded in comedy. The authors also refer to what W. E. B. Du Bois called "double-consciousness" or "two-ness." Because you are "other," you have a different perspective, the ability to see how you fit into our complicated American tapestry. Standing on the margins, you have the perspective to understand the bigger picture. Humor requires a deep awareness of culture and human nature. You see dichotomies and contradictions. The alienation gives you a unique perspective. As a person who is bicultural, I find this makes complete sense. So much of my writing, worldview, and sense of humor is based on the discomfort of being fractured. I've often had to consider who I am in many contexts, particularly white ones. There is a saying in Spanish: Ni de aquí, ni de allá, "From neither here nor there." It's something many of us say when we feel we don't belong in either culture. Unfortunately, this was popularized by La India María, a fictional and stereotypical Mexican character who should be an embarrassment to us as a people. Yeesh.

I've always felt out of place wherever I go. I understood my identity as an outsider very early on, and my way of handling it has always been through writing and laughing about my experiences. Growing up, I always felt like a pariah, a misfit, and a disappointment in my traditional Mexican family and community. I was a foul-mouthed feminist rabble-rouser who dressed in black and was always getting into altercations when I perceived any kind of injustice. (I once took a Jehovah's Witness in my school to Boystown, the gay neighborhood in Chicago, just to prove a point. I dared him with my eyes to say some shit.) Then, as I grew older, I was often one of the few people of color in professional settings, many times the only Mexican. So much of my humor is born from a sense of alienation, which is true of a lot of comedians. That's why they're always such miserable bastards.

I admit that I love to make racial jokes. And I love making them in front of white people, who squirm at the mere mention of even the most innocuous reference to race. The discomfort on their faces brings me such satisfaction. Honestly, I see it as a kind of reparation. Years ago, a white man I worked with was harmlessly discussing our Black coworker when I looked him straight in the face and said, defensively, "Oh, you mean the *Black* guy?" He looked terrified, mortified that his efforts to skirt this very detail were being exposed. He probably thought I was going to report him to HR, until I burst out laughing. Maybe I'm a terrible person.

Freud believed that humor was a way for people to defeat their inhibitions, ease psychological stress, and manifest their suppressed fears and desires. Is that why I go out of my way to make white people feel uncomfortable? Do I like to see them suffer? Is it a way for me to express how I feel about being a person of color in such a racist society? And what would Freud say about my queef jokes? Do I secretly like queefing? Do I fear it? #DeepThoughts

I talk, write, and joke about what's wrong with me, which is a lot of things. I'm hella moody and snide, I'm way too sensitive, my ears are teeny-tiny, I'm easily distracted, I'm disorganized, I hold (and nurse) grudges, I have a bad temper, and I have a widow's peak that rivals Eddie Munster's. Also, I'm prone to reaching George Costanza levels of pettiness. (Fuck you, Professor Hofer.) Laziness is another one of my flaws, and as anyone struggling with it can attest, it often prevents you from being your best self. This unfortunate truth was on display when I accidentally knocked my roommate's toothbrush into the toilet while attending a summer writing workshop when I was fifteen. My solution was to fish it out, rinse it off, and put it back. Why did I do this? I didn't feel like going into town to buy her a new one. It was too far. It's not that I didn't like her, it's that I didn't want to deal with the inconvenience.

I've lived with depression since I was a kid. I suspect I was already having existential crises in my mother's uterus. Ridiculing my mental illness makes it less powerful to me. Sometimes I refer to my depressive episodes or anxiety attacks as "the crazies" and tell my loved ones that I have to knock my ass out with some pills so I can learn how to be a person again. Mental illness is not something that Mexicans freely discuss, but I find it liberating to own it and control the narrative. (As a result, I'm the person in the family others confess their mental illnesses to. Fun!) Finding humor in things that drive me to despair invites nuance and complexity into episodes that are otherwise full of only pain. I like to joke about the job that literally made me suicidal when I was in my early thirties, for example. In 2014, I had a job in public relations that required me to frequently travel to New York. My boss was a controlling nutsack. The pressure of the job obliterated my mental health. I was so depressed that getting up to get a glass of water seemed pointless. Fuck you, water! I was practically catatonic for a few months, spending hours a day watching *Gilmore Girls*. I can't help but laugh when I look back on it and consider that I thought of ways to kill myself while Sookie St. James cheerfully made a frittata or some shit.

Sometimes my honesty makes people uncomfortable, and so does my sense of humor. One of my greatest fears in life is to be raped. I have been assaulted in countless ways, and men have definitely *tried* to rape me, but it's never happened, which feels like some kind of miracle. What a sad thing to celebrate. So I joke about this fear. A lot. And I know this is hard to believe, but not everyone loves rape jokes. Though it may seem offensive and maybe a little disturbing, I do this to deal with the dangers of having a vagina, of having to constantly evaluate people and situations according to how scary I find them. One drunken night, my friend and I came up with what we call the Rapey Scale.

Take, for instance, the finance guy I met for drinks one night who was intent on getting me drunk and taking me to his apartment nearby, claiming he was "the perfect gentleman." I give that a seven. He really put in some work, until I ran away and got in a cab. Then there was my boyfriend's friend when we were fifteen. He was trying to lure me into a bedroom to "lie down and rest" at a daytime high school party when I was incredibly drunk. That feels like an eight. The two men who violently groped me as I drunkenly wandered through a club I snuck into at seventeen? That's a nine. I had to fight them off and no one helped me. Then there was the boyfriend when I was in my thirties who repeatedly pressured me to have sex in a position that made me gasp in pain, one that I specifically told him made me feel violated. Nine? And then there's the time a man followed me at night making sucking noises until I ran inside my house. Feels like a nine to me. What about the boy who violently grabbed me by the crotch as I walked down the hall at school when I was six? That one's tough. Most definitely rapey, but the boy was also six, and where the fuck did he learn that? Should I give that a seven? I was so afraid but told no one. . . . And so on and so forth. You get the picture.

You know what's getting really fucking old? Arguing about whether women are funny. Are we done with that yet? Because yes, we are hilarious. Whether men enjoy our humor is another story. How could we not be funny living in this gross, misogynist world? We're not taking it all in stride, let me tell you.

I think the discomfort that people feel about my honesty and humor has much to do with whether I, as a woman, have permission to be irreverent or funny. Women are not often encouraged to be funny, because comedy is considered aggressive, masculine, and threatening. It's unladylike to be smart and talk about "inappropriate" things. Personally, I will not hesitate to discuss sex or bodily functions, but I know some men find this quality unattractive, and I understand that it's not every woman's jam. And there are plenty of men out there with the sense of humor of a garden slug. Gender ain't got nothing to do with it.

There's a theory, based on evolutionary psychology, that men try harder to get laid and humor is instrumental in this effort. According to this theory, humor demonstrates a man's intelligence, which makes him a more appealing mate. Women have to be selective in choosing our partners, because motherhood is no fucking joke and we need reliable mates to increase the chances of our babies' survival. So the funnier a man is, the more likely he is to get laid. Makes sense, I guess, but it bums me out. Is there no biological reason for women to be funny?

A study conducted at McMaster University and published in 2006 in *Evolution and Human Behavior* suggests that women's sense of humor is unimportant to men. In this study, psychologists Eric Bressler and Sigal Balshine showed 210 college students pictures of "two equally attractive members of the opposite sex," as stated in an article on Science.org. Under the photographs, they included statements, supposedly authored by the person pictured, that were either funny or not funny. According to the findings, female participants desired a funny man, while the men didn't give three shits about the women's funniness. In another study conducted later that year, Bressler and Balshine again found that the men preferred someone who thought *they* were funny. I was incredulous about what the results suggested, so I asked my ex-husband about it before we divorced—I trusted his opinion despite our circumstance, maybe even because of it—and he confirmed this preference. He didn't care if his partner was funny. He just wanted a good audience. Good to know.

But what about the oft-cited idea that humor makes a woman seem less threatening and more socially attractive? Why is it that men are so often either indifferent or intimidated by funny women?

Christopher Hitchens, the world-renowned grouse and "intellectual," notoriously argued that women aren't funny because it scares men. Our smarts turn their pee-pees inside out or something. Hitchens admitted, however, that there were *some* decent female comedians, but most of them were "hefty or dykey or Jewish, or some combo of the three." Rest in peace, but seriously, what a dick. The argument is so boring and stupid that it makes me want to eat biscuits in a fit of rage until I pass out. What seems just as likely is that women are underrepresented in comedy because of what I like to call Thousands of Years of Misogyny and Sexism. But what do I know? I'm just a Mexican.

TWO OF MY PATERNAL AUNTS are the funniest women I've ever known, so I never considered that women weren't funny. I watched them as a child, fascinated by their quick retorts and absurd versions of small-town gossip. This was how I learned to tell spicy stories and make people laugh. Tía Tere is sharp-witted and loves to tell ridiculous stories. She's the one who shared the tale of La Culpa. Her retorts are always precise and cutting. When a member of the family was being rude, she asked him to please stop behaving so "Ku Klux Klan." At a party a few years ago, she made a joke about panochas that made my mom laugh so hard it made me uncomfortable. (Like most humans, I don't ever want to associate my mother with sex. Even saying so has me dry-heaving and shuddering as I write.) Then there is Tía Blanca, who will not leave anyone or anything unscathed. You can't have an ego in her presence because she'll cut you down in the most hilarious and creative way possible. She is a tough broad with a foul mouth who never married because, in her words, she didn't like men telling her what to do. My favorite Tía Blanca story is the time she was sharpening knives outside when a man walked past catcalling any woman within earshot. Tía Blanca was so enraged that she threw a knife at him. He was not hurt, but she made her point. Needless to say, I admire her life choices.

Tía Blanca lived with us for a time in the early '90s and it was memorable. I was about six and my brother was about eleven. Sometimes we'd watch *The Price Is Right* together. Whenever a contestant on the show didn't follow the advice that she shouted at the TV, she automatically labeled them "un pinche pendejo hijo de su puta madre." And she was right. They were.

My two brothers are the biggest trolls who've ever lived, and whenever the three of us get together, we mostly focus on finding clever ways to embarrass each other. This dynamic is the reason that I search for humor in all things. It's become a defense mechanism, a weapon, a source of joy. If we can laugh about something, it hurts less.

When my little brother tried to grow a sad little mustache, it was a whole scene. We still talk about it. I have always been teased for my very large mouth. I mean this literally—I have huge lips and teeth to match. Once I asked my older brother to hand me a spoon and, with a straight face, he gave me a ladle. Motherfucker got me good. My little brother was once judging me for one of my terrible relationships. He hated my ex and was disappointed I had made such a poor choice. "He was handsome!" I said in my defense. "You know who else was handsome?" he replied. "Ted Bundy."

He won. Respect.

Everyone and everything is up for grabs when we join forces. One of our running jokes, thanks to my older brother, is that greyhound dogs "look racist." I urge you to consider this next time you see one—it's truly uncanny. They really look like they would call ICE and ruin your cookout. Most of our group texts consist of us talking shit about white people, particularly their unseasoned foods and penchant for walking barefoot in public places. There are times when the three of us laugh like fools while the rest of the family, particularly my niece and nephew, look at us like we're demented.

How else can we live in this white supremacist society without becoming bitter? Humor makes it all a little more bearable. If I came out of every racist encounter I've ever had tearful and defeated, I would not have made it this far, of that I am certain. White supremacy is funny because it is stupid; it makes no goddamn sense. Basically, you're telling me that Stephen Miller is inherently superior to me? That bitch looks like a gland.

I WAS A MELANCHOLIC KID, but I loved comedy. It was one of my few pleasures in life and it kept me afloat. It was often my brief break from depression. I looked forward to *Saturday Night Live* all week. Chris Farley spinning around and smashing into tables just about killed me. Just looking at Will Ferrell's ridiculous face was enough to send me into hysterics. Molly Shannon was also one of my favorites, especially when she played the armpit-sniffing, tree-groping Mary Katherine Gallagher. She was so animated, so unapologetically gross and silly. Once I even wrote an acrostic poem about Norm Macdonald, who I revered as the master of sarcasm.

In grade school, I had a best friend named Claudia. Era igual de hocicona, so I was intrigued by her. We were both going through a lot at home, but rarely ever talked about it. Our families were challenging and sometimes suffocating, so we took refuge in each other. Of course, at the time, I didn't make all these connections. I thought we were just two weird little girls who liked to read, build things out of garbage, and make fun of people. Together we were the snarkiest fuckers who ever lived. To get through the day we tried to crack each other up any way possible—funny faces, impressions, ruthless observations. Nothing was off-limits. I will admit that I peed my pants a little bit on more than one occasion. (In the process of writing this essay I begin to realize that perhaps I had a medical problem.) In fifth grade, Claudia made me laugh so hard that I had to leave the class and stay in the bathroom until I calmed down. I remember my face was bright red when I looked in the mirror. I felt like a ding-dong, but the laughter kept welling inside my chest and flooding out of my mouth.

In eighth grade, Claudia and I were once again reunited in homeroom, and we still had not matured except that we now had boobs. We continued laughing at everything and the class turned into a total free-for-all. Our teacher, Mrs. Sellner, was a white lady in her forties who had just received her teaching degree, and I can imagine that being suddenly in charge of a classroom of poor Mexican kids was somewhat of a culture shock. We could smell her inexperience and acted accordingly. From the moment she entered our lives she was known as "Sellnerd." Brilliant, I know.

We were pretty feral that year, probably as a result of our rapidly shifting hormones. We were loud and deranged most of the time. There was a boy named Pedro, possibly the gayest boy I have ever met, who would dance on his desk like Madonna whenever our teachers left the classroom. Claudia threw books out the window for no reason at all. Kids flung crap at each other and got into fistfights.

When Sellnerd came back from winter break in Jamaica with her thin, wispy hair in cornrows, Claudia and I looked at each other and lost our fucking minds.

Did I mention we were assholes?

I HAD ANOTHER group of friends in junior high who could be best described as a gaggle of misfits. We were dorky girls who would spend recess quoting *The Simpsons* and roasting everyone, including each other. Jenny was overweight and very self-conscious about it. Her family life was mysterious, but I did know her father was an abusive drug addict. We were friends with her for years and never once stepped inside her house. One of Jenny's recurring bits was about *Alf* (the hit TV show from the '90s about an alien living with a suburban family) and the eponymous character's appetite for cats. Nadia was a skinny girl with big eyes and gigantic gums and protruding teeth (later treated by braces) who hated her mother with a fervor I couldn't quite understand. She was obsessed with Marilyn Manson and would sarcastically destroy anyone who even looked in our direction. Then there was Vanessa, who was the most normal and well-adjusted. She had a loving family and a positive outlook on life. The only thing strange about her was that she was short, like, *for real* short. And I, of course, was a deeply depressed smart-ass. I painted my nails black and loved disco-inspired clothing for reasons I still can't understand. I wore a lot of polyester, which is a poor choice when you're going through puberty and your sweat glands are out of control.

Trauma or alienation had brought us together, and we laughed in spite of it . . . or because of it; it's hard to say. Those moments in which we lost our shit over Kermit the Frog or some kid in our class who looked like an armadillo were pure bliss, some of the best moments of my sad teenage existence.

I watched *The Simpsons* every weekday, sometimes multiple times a day, from the ages of five to seventeen. Since I was prone to sulking and brooding, my parents were pleased to see me laugh for the duration of the episodes. I thought the show was brilliant and loved its irreverence toward the world. It taught me to revel in absurdity and brought me comfort like nothing else could. Lisa Simpson was the first feminist icon I had come across. I wanted to be just like her, except slightly less annoying. I had *The Simpsons* T-shirts, posters, toys, and action figures. It remains my most long-lasting and codependent relationship. I used the show to gauge a person's intelligence and general likability. Whoever thought it was crass and juvenile was dead to me, essentially.

AT A VERY TENDER AGE I decided I wanted to be tough and talk shit.

I was about thirteen when I watched Janeane Garofalo perform stand-up. For a few years my family had an illegal hot-box (seriously, that's what it was called), so we were able to get free cable. To our chagrin, companies caught on and they became obsolete shortly after we began using them. During the brief era of the Sánchez family hot-box, Comedy Central became one of my favorite channels, and I would watch reruns of stand-up specials over and over again because I had few friends and nothing better to do.

Janeane Garofalo instantly became my idol. I loved how edgy and cool she was in that '90s sort of way, with her red shorts, black tights, and chunky black shoes. Though she was self-deprecating, she exuded the kind of confidence I wanted. She knew exactly who she was and didn't say she was sorry. *I want to be like her*, I thought to myself. *I want to be funny and strong.*

IN THE AFOREMENTIONED Chris Rock interview, he points out that comedians are acutely aware of damn near everything. "Being a comedian," he explains, "80 percent of the job is just you notice shit, which is a trait of schizophrenics, too. You notice things people don't notice." A 2014 study published by the University of Oxford finds that the features of the brain that induce the creativity necessary for humor are remarkably similar to those that induce psychiatric illnesses such as schizophrenia and bipolar disorder. In a BBC article published in 2014, Professor Gordon Claridge posits that mania can encourage people to come up with new ideas and form compelling and funny connections.

I can see the same logic applying to writers. We notice a lot of things other people don't. We have to constantly pay attention to the world around us if we want to say anything new or interesting.

Incidentally, many (most?) poets I know have experienced some sort of mental illness. We are a frail group of people. If you're a comedic writer, you might be doubly fucked. I wouldn't label myself as such, but I care deeply about both comedy and writing, and I notice the dumbest shit. I don't feel sorry for myself, but this kind of seeing, sensibility, or whatever you want to call it does feel like an illness at times. A dead bird will ruin my day. An abandoned dildo on a sidewalk will have me musing for hours. A woman's shoe left behind in a bar will send me into a fit of giggles. Carriage horses draped in dirty velvet make me weep. The false dignity of such beautiful creatures breaks my heart.

Why can't I just go about my day like a normal American—stuff my face with hydrogenated fats and fall asleep watching *The Real Housewives of Wherever-the-Fuck*?

PEOPLE ARE OFTEN surprised by my foul mouth. I think some find this quality of mine so shocking because I'm little and Brown and look like I should be quietly taking care of your children or cleaning your house. For the most part, I'm a friendly person, but my mouth . . . it's street. Every other sentence ends with "'n' shit." And if you piss me off, I become a fountain of vicious insults. It's best not to cross me, because I will delight in your insecurities. I'm not always great at being "the bigger person." (For what, really? Yuck.)

The trouble with my mouth started early. In first grade, my teacher threatened to wash my mouth with soap because I said the word "fart." I didn't understand why it was a bad word—I still don't—and so I was stunned by her anger. Throughout my childhood my mom threatened to slap me across the mouth because she didn't like what was coming out of it. In high school, I was always in the principal's office for talking shit to teachers who were conservative or dim-witted (often both) and who I therefore didn't respect. For better or worse, I've never had trouble speaking my mind.

MY TENTH-GRADE ENGLISH TEACHER, Mr. Antus, a Vietnam vet with PTSD who looked exactly like Burt Reynolds, used to tell us that sarcastic people didn't have many friends. At the time I thought he was ridiculous, but I soon learned that he was right.

When I was twenty-two and dated Abdul (who I called Mr. Pakistani Man), I learned this was true. One night he made a reference to Muslim stereotypes, and I sarcastically responded with something like, "Well, you know how *those* people are." I never imagined he would believe that I was serious. Of course I wasn't xenophobic or racist. Plus, I loved him, or so I thought. He was furious, though. Damn. I thought he was used to my sardonic personality, but I was way off. I apologized profusely and explained that it was said without any particular details of how "those people" are in mind, but he wasn't having any of it. I spent hours crying and begging for forgiveness.

IN THE SPRING of 2010, with our economy deep in the shitter, I completed graduate school. Though I knew life would not be easy with a degree in poetry (pendeja), I never imagined how hard it would be to get a job. I ended up at a marketing firm in the Sears Tower, where I languished for two miserable years. (Please note that Chicagoans would rather drink river water than acknowledge this building as the "Willis Tower.") My title there was "print estimator," which was as boring as it sounds. This was a terrible, terrible time in my life. Some mornings I was so depressed that I would literally gag on my way to work. At times I would look around my cubicle and wonder, *Is this really what my life has become?* Had I been a ruthless killer in a past life?

At work, I often chatted online with my friend Michael to help me get through the day. Our conversations were always nonsensical and inappropriate, and looking back, I'm surprised by how brazen I was to talk so much shit on my work computer. For a while, we had a side project outside of our work lives, a podcast titled *Oh Hells Nah*, in which we mostly insulted each other and went on bizarre tangents. We always found a way to mention "butt-to-butt," a sex act that I'd seen in a soft-core Cinemax film in a hotel room in Nicaragua several years prior. In the scene, two characters gently rubbed their butts together, true to the term we coined. Michael had not seen this with his own eyes, but he was delighted by the idea, and for a time, "butt-to-butt" was our favorite thing to say. It quickly got on everyone's nerves, but we carried on because we were trailblazers.

On that particular day, Michael and I started chatting about the Duggars, an evangelical family who had their own reality TV show for having an obscene amount of children. Inevitably, the mom's vagina came up. We pondered what it looked like after shooting out nineteen kids. Among other things, Michael called it "a wind tunnel" and "a hungry gaping maw." I simply described it as "all flappy and shit." I don't know why, probably because I was supposed to be busy estimating the cost of posters, but I started laughing about the Duggar vagina and couldn't stop.

I disrupted my coworker Frank, who sat in the cubicle next to me, my only friend in that godforsaken place. I was twenty-six and he was a fiftysomething Italian guy, so we were a weird lunch-time pair. Frank peeked his head over the partition and asked what the hell was going on. We were always laughing together and he wanted in on it. My stomach muscles ached and my face was hot. I kept trying to tell him about the flappy vagina, but as soon as I did, I ended up laughing again. This went on for several minutes, me trying and failing to explain it. He was dumbfounded, probably thought I needed to be committed to an asylum or shot with a tranquilizer. Somehow I had sense enough to worry that one of the managers would come out and see me in this unhinged state. And that the sight of this Brown girl doing anything but working hard would be cause enough for a firing or other reprimand, so I escorted myself to the bathroom and tried to laugh it out like I had when I was a kid. After some time had passed, I was able to tell Frank about the Duggar mom. I used my hand to simulate the flapping.

THIS IS GONNA get me canceled, excommunicated, shunned, ostracized, or whatever, but I think some feminists are humorless, and they bum me out. I'm down with the cause, consider myself a strong and shrill feminist shrew, but some of my sisters are tedious and bent on sucking the fun out of everything. If, for instance, I can't make fun of the Duggar mom's sloppy Republican vagina, I don't want to be a part of your movement.

George Carlin, one of the most brilliant comedians of all time, has one of the best stand-up openings about antichoice women. Every single time I watch it, I let out a yelp. I know if this were performed today, people on the internet would be outraged. With no context whatsoever, Carlin asks the following question: "Why is it that most women who are against abortion are people you wouldn't want to fuck in the first place?"

I have no interest in being a perfect feminist role model, because not only is that impossible, it's boring as fuck. And anyway, the consensus seems to be that I didn't make the cut. I've been accused of not being feminist enough for a number of perplexing reasons: I'm too feminine; I support things that objectify women (I once went to a porn expo on assignment); I expect men to pay for dinner (Wage gap. Ever heard of it?). I also have no problem using my physical appearance to get ahead (You want to be nice to me because I'm pretty? What the fuck do I care?).

I often find criticism amusing and conflict rife with opportunities for intellectual exploration. That's why when people ask me why I don't write about happiness, I stare at them blankly like a chicken. For me, the best creative expression is born of tension.

I've heard feminists criticize Amy Schumer for her self-deprecating humor, accusing her of catering to men and being self-loathing. To that I say, you're missing the point. Schumer, while obviously ignorant about race—often to a cringeworthy degree—is not afraid to tread on uncomfortable territory when it comes to gender, and I appreciate that about her. In one episode of her show, *Inside Amy Schumer,* written as a parody of *12 Angry Men,* twelve jurors deliberate over whether Schumer is hot enough to be on TV. If they decide she is not, she will lose her show and possibly be put to death. One of the jurors calls her a "potato face," and another says she looks like a chipmunk. After that episode, I remember a lot of feminists on Twitter insisting that Schumer was pandering to men by making fun of her own appearance, which I found to be a tired and simplistic argument.

It's not that Schumer believes she's ugly, it's that she's ridiculing men who lambaste women's physical appearance. It's particularly funny that most of the jurors in the skit are not at all fuckable. That's called *subversion,* folks. Fuck, once you explain a joke it ceases to be funny. Thanks a lot, feminists. Look what you've made me do.

I'll be damned if I can't make fun of myself. I love my giant mouth, but I will still make jokes about it. I don't believe in phrenology, but I will refer to my propensity for amorousness manifested in my skull shape whenever the fuck I want. I find your movement oppressive if I can't laugh at the silliness of being a human being. Might as well lie down on a heap of soiled mattresses on the street and die.

WHEN I LIVED in Spain at the age of twenty-two on a Fulbright, I met a hilarious Tunisian man at a friend's birthday party and began dating him shortly after. He had been living in Madrid for years and spoke perfect Spanish. Nearly everything that came out of his mouth was a joke. It won me over from the start. I guess those scientists were right about jokes causing lady-boners.

Though I had grown up bilingual, I found that I simply wasn't as funny in Spain. I had spoken Spanish my entire life, but the vast majority of my education had been in English, and therefore my English vocabulary was much broader. Also, so much of my humor depended on shared cultural experiences. When I got to Spain, I was unfamiliar with the culture, and I continued to speak Mexican Spanish because I didn't want to be a pretentious Eurocentric asshole and feel like a traitor to my family. What this meant, though, was that my wit was not as sharp in Spanish society. Spaniards weren't familiar with my Mexican references, my Mexican sensibility. Nor did they understand what it was like to grow up in the '90s in Chicago. The same applied to my Tunisian boyfriend. So either I kept my jokes to myself or they fell flat. I felt like part of my identity had been taken away. I was used to being the jokester in my relationships and this was disorienting.

"I'm funny!" I wanted to scream and violently shake him by his lapels. "I swear to God I'm funny! You're not the only one who is funny!"

SOMETIMES I LAUGH harder at my jokes than anyone else. I should be embarrassed by this, but I'm not. I wouldn't have said it if I didn't think it was funny. I laugh all the time when I'm alone, which is often. It confuses or troubles strangers, but I'm totally OK with that. I consider laughing at my own jokes a sort of gift to myself. My inner monologues are very entertaining.

The relationship we have with ourselves is the most important relationship we will ever have, and yet no one talks about it. We are conditioned to be afraid of solitude, of being alone with our thoughts. We fill our lives with screens and noise so we don't have to live with the silence when no one else is around. This is particularly true for women. The time I spent as a washed-up, divorced woman in her thirties, before finding real love and becoming a mother, was proof of this. Everywhere I went, everyone wanted to know where my husband was.

ONE OF THE REASONS I left my ex-husband—and there were many—is because he began to look past me, like I wasn't even there. We met in grad school in 2007. First we dated, then we lived together, and then we got married when we were both thirty years old. Our marriage lasted only a year and a half. We were never meant for each other, and I think we both knew it deep inside. It was like putting on a pair of shoes two sizes too small and hobbling around like that for eight years. We had such different approaches to life. He didn't know how to be my husband and I didn't know how to be his wife.

I'd like to believe there was no villain, that we were simply mismatched and both of us insisted on making it work because we did love each other in a sense, until it was all too much. I eventually unraveled. Maybe he thinks otherwise. I don't know. I still have affection for him and the time we spent together. Leaving him was one of the hardest things I've ever done, but I knew in my body that I had to.

What hurt the most at the end was his indifference toward me. He no longer laughed at my jokes, he said, because he was used to my sense of humor. I didn't surprise him anymore; I had lost my charm. My self-esteem took quite a hit because I'd always thought my humor made me special. Sometimes he thought I was too crass, particularly when a joke involved sex or poop, which was often. If he responded at all, it was a half-hearted "uh-huh," just to acknowledge that I had spoken. I don't believe myself to be a reiteration of Richard Pryor, but I've made people hurt themselves with laughter. Something had been broken.

STUDIES HAVE SHOWN that even rats laugh, which makes me feel conflicted about my deep fear and hatred of them. In 1997, a psychologist and his student conducted an experiment in which they tickled rats to see if they chirped differently. Not only did they emit a distinct chirp, the rats pressed themselves against their fingers for more tickling. This would almost be cute if rats weren't so disgusting. But if rats laugh, other animals must laugh, too. The thought of a laughing baby sea otter gives me so much irrational hope and happiness that it makes me want to kick a table over.

THE DAY I MOVED OUT of the apartment I'd shared with my ex-husband and into my own, I went grocery shopping with a friend as a newly separated woman. Shopping for myself felt odd. I kept reaching for items my ex-husband would want, then pulling my hand back when I realized he was gone. I bought things that I knew he would disapprove of. Flavored sparkling water? Why the fuck not? Throughout the process, I felt an overwhelming sadness that we would never again shop for groceries together, that I didn't have to remember to get him pickles.

After the grocery store, my friend and I headed to the dollar store to buy some household items. We were delighted to get a candle or a pair of scissors for the low, low price of one American dollar. What a time to be alive! We walked around packing our baskets to the brim, joking about how much we were loving the mundane errand.

As we carried our spoils to my car, I turned to my friend and said, "Just two single ladies in their thirties enjoying their Sunday night at the dollar store." It wasn't that funny, but we both laughed at the absurdity of our joy in buying cheap knickknacks.

Sunday nights usually fill me with a quiet bleakness, but that night, I laughed at the state of my life. I felt relief. It was February and the snow had briefly thawed. It almost smelled like spring.

BACK TO THE
MOTHERLAND

I come from a long line of peasants. We are a hearty desert people. Scrappy motherfuckers. I'm reminded of this every time I
return to northern Mexico and study the Sierra Madre landscape.
The land does not yield or forgive. According to colonial Spanish
accounts, the climate in this region was so extreme that unprotected horses were susceptible to freezing in the winter. The summer months brought a heat so intense that Spaniards claimed it
rivaled Africa's.

I've asked my family again and again about the Indigenous civ-
ilization we descended from, but no one can give me a definite
answer. We are poor rural Mexicans, and thus muddled beyond
simple classification. There is a great-great-great-grandfather (or
some shit) who was Spanish, but that's all I've been able to un-
earth. The best I can do is assume that based on where my family
hails from, part of our ancestry is Tepehuan Indian. I want to believe this because the Tepehuanes were fierce. Tired of overwork
and mistreatment, they revolted against the Spanish in 1616, an

uprising that the colonizers never saw coming. Andrés Pérez de Ribas, a Jesuit historian and contemporary of the time, described it as "one of the greatest outbreaks of disorder, upheaval, and destruction that had been seen in New Spain . . . since the Conquest." They fought the Spanish for *four brutal years*.

My family members on both sides have a wide medley of pigments—from pasty white to dark brown. Blue, green, and brown eyes. Red, blond, black, and brown hair. When I hear people say that a person doesn't "look Mexican," I'd like to show them a family portrait and suggest they read a history book. Sometimes people tell me this as if it's some sort of compliment. Oh, I can pass for Italian or Greek, they assure me. Bitch, no. Whatever you're trying to say by that, I don't want it. A man hitting on me at a bar once told me I had a "very interesting nose" and wanted to know where I was from. When I told him I was Mexican, I must have shattered his exotic fantasy, because he looked disappointed. I suppose my origins were too pedestrian for his erotic imagination. People often ask me where I'm from, and when I say Chicago, they look perplexed. One man told me I didn't look like it. I suppose he had never in his life been to Chicago because, come on, I can throw my chancla in any direction and hit a nice señora who wishes me a good day.

And then there are those who hesitate to use the word "Mexican" because they think it's a pejorative term. Instead they say "Spanish" or "Latin." They whisper "Mexican" as if it was an embarrassing diagnosis, and I, exasperated, want to yell, "Bitch, he is *literally* Mexican! From Mexico! He told me with his mouth!"

. . .

MY WHOLE LIFE, I fantasized about living in an unfamiliar land where I would frantically write until the sun came up. That's what I imagined a writer's life to be—full of adventure, booze, cigarettes, sex, and faded black clothing. I constructed this romantic bohemian image from the movies I'd seen and the books I'd read, and in a sense, I made it come true.

I was the first woman on my mom's side of the family to attend college, and if my parents were offended by what they saw as my premature departure from home, leaving the country was almost unspeakable. Why in the world would I want to fend for myself? And now I was moving across the ocean? For what? Who did I think I was?

But what they considered an ordinary life, one filled with the drudgery of typical social conventions and obligations, seemed like a slow, excruciating death to me. I didn't want a stable office job after college. I didn't want to get married and have kids. I didn't want to be a responsible adult who wore slacks to work and cared about her 401(k) (I just learned what this is; I'm a failure of an adult). Instead, I longed for a strange, impossible life entirely of my own design. I had long since decided this was my destiny, even if nothing in the world had ever suggested it was possible.

I originally planned to apply for a Fulbright in a more obscure country like Uruguay (I knew absolutely nothing about Uruguay), because I didn't believe that I could get a scholarship to Spain, which I imagined was a popular and thus competitive choice. My friends, however, coaxed me into trying. What did I have to lose except my pride?

When I told some Mexicans about my upcoming year in Spain, many were impressed that I was going back to "the motherland." I was excited to understand some of my origins, but to call this place my motherland was an insult to my brown-skinned mother. What did Spain have to do with me?

I arrived in Madrid a breathless and eager twenty-two-year-old adding to my family's list of firsts, travel across the Atlantic. The city overwhelmed me, which is exactly what I was searching for. I was restless and seeking constant stimulation. I wanted loud music, disco balls, and bright lights to follow me everywhere I went. I dove into the nightlife at full force. There was a collective exuberance in the city that I had never experienced. Bengali men sold roses and flashing knickknacks on street corners. Chinese women hawked beers and sandwiches to drunkards spilling out of bars. The throngs of people excited me, and I was delighted that even the elderly were out at all hours, stumbling about after too many glasses of wine. *These people really know how to live*, I thought to myself. Americans were doing it all wrong.

Calle de la Montera, which was right in the center of the city, was a spectacle. I grew up with a grimy motel on the corner of my block and was accustomed to seeing sex workers sell their wares, but Calle de la Montera was something else entirely. It was as if the whole world were represented by women—some young and beautiful, others old and withered, some cis, some trans—in varying degrees of undress on a single street. They lined the sidewalks announcing their services, their bodies provocatively poised for work. It was one of the most diverse places I had ever seen in my life. The police stood idly by, unfazed by the transactions, an unspoken understanding. I tried not to gawk, but I was fascinated and always found reasons to walk down that stretch. I admired the hustle of the workers and judged the men who solicited them. They were crude and I hated the way they spoke to the women, as if they were disposable, as if everything humanly possible had a monetary price.

At twenty-two, I found that sex was at the forefront of my mind, and I quickly learned of my own sexual capital upon my arrival. Spanish men were almost indifferent to me, which was fine—they didn't wet my whistle either—but when I walked down the street, the swarthy immigrants would lavish attention on me, alternately complimenting and harassing me. Depending on my mood, and if it wasn't too aggressive, there were times I enjoyed it. I was young and excited about my burgeoning sexuality. There was something fun and exhilarating about wielding that sort of power, the power of being desired. When I stared back at them, I tried to look insolent, almost mocking. I was trying to challenge them to follow through with their catcalls. It was not surprising that it was all talk; most of them became flustered and did nothing.

I wasn't technically single, however. I was still in love with the married man in Chicago. I called Abdul my boyfriend despite how ridiculous it sounded in those circumstances. But what else could

I call him? My lover? I can't say that word with a straight face. The hot foreign dude I was having an affair with? The man who emotionally abused me from across an ocean?

Even more absurd was my promise to be faithful to him. I was stupidly, savagely, irrationally enamored with this man even though I knew he would never belong to me. I also promised him I wouldn't eat pork, because despite his obvious transgressions, he still considered himself a devout Muslim. But the swine beckoned me everywhere I went—glistening pork legs hung from ceiling hooks in nearly every bar and restaurant. I broke my promise within weeks—pig was so salty and delicious. And who was he to keep me from dirty animal meats when he had a wife?

I could never get full that year. I wanted to taste everything. I ate so many tortillas españolas that all these years later, I still can't eat them without feeling a little bit ill. Egg on a baguette paired with creamy coffee was unbelievably satisfying, and I couldn't get enough. It was as if I were descosida—unstitched—a word my mother uses to describe my gluttony. I crammed my face with every kind of food and guzzled wine like it was water. Bottles were only two euros apiece; I could afford as much alcohol as I wished. All my life, I'd been filled with desire, and at last I was able to feed it.

When I was a kid, my family lived in a back apartment that faced an alley. The building was a two-flat that had been illegally converted into four units. We were separated from our neighbors next door by sheets of plywood nailed to the wall. My mother worked nights, and my dad, exhausted after work, was usually on the sofa watching TV. Because my brother was five years older, we rarely played together. I was 100 percent the annoying little sister. Think Lisa Simpson but super depressed.

I spent so much of my childhood alone—reading, drawing, and looking out the window. There were times I was so desperate for companionship that I called a toll-free number to listen to a re- cording of a story. How pitiful and hilarious that I relied on an automated voice to get me through the day.

Our living room window faced north and there was a tree in the distance that always enchanted me. I thought it was so beauti- ful and I wanted so much to be there, to be elsewhere. It seemed so far and inaccessible, but now I realize it couldn't have been more than a few blocks away. Though there was nothing special about it, the tree became an emblem of my escape, of what was possible.

When I was eleven, we moved into our first house, which was in the same town of Cicero, but in a better neighborhood. There were still some white people on the street at the time, and one of them slashed our tires one night. We had infiltrated their sad little pocket. By the time I was in high school, white people were increas- ingly rare and often impoverished. Some assimilated to us so much they became almost Mexican.

In the evenings, my best friend, Claudia, and I would walk to karate lessons on Roosevelt Road, which was technically in Chi- cago proper, but only a few blocks away. Occasionally, we took de- tours and explored the industrial areas in the neighborhood. Claudia always wanted to push boundaries, and I did, too, though I was often scared and would complain I had a stomachache. Once, we snuck into an abandoned factory. I worried that there were homeless people or drug addicts lurking in dark corners ready to murder us, but I pressed on because my curiosity was stronger than my terror. The building had been damaged in a fire—the second floor was soft and crumbling, ready to cave in, but we still walked across it.

We found a tree growing inside the first floor. Light poured through a hole in the roof, illuminating it like a miracle. I thought it was amazing, but fear still ran through me like a spike.

My behavior, the desire to always get entangled in some kind of mess, to reach beyond what I am allowed, has always been considered unfeminine in traditional Mexican culture. My maternal grandmother often called me "marimacha," which translates to "butch" or "dyke." My mother, much less harsh, called me "andariega," which means "wanderer," or "callejera," which means "woman of the streets."

Girls are not supposed to stray from their homes.

I RENTED MY first apartment in a ritzy part of Madrid, much too far from the school where I worked as a teaching assistant. I didn't know anything about the city and took an apartment that seemed clean and near some nightlife. Had I known how dull and pretentious the neighborhood would be, I would have chosen a different location, because what I really wanted was noise and grime. I wanted to feel at home.

I shared the place with a motley of girls, two of whom were studying abroad. One of them was a grouchy Spanish girl who would sleep late into the afternoon. There was something about her face that I didn't like.

I loved the romance of the balcony off my bedroom that looked out onto the street. I took many selfies (before they were called "selfies") in front of the giant window looking all pensive and shit. I felt the need to document every part of my life because I couldn't believe that I was living it. There was nothing particularly memorable about the apartment besides the lumpy mattress that made me feel like I was sleeping on a sack of dead cats.

Soon after moving in, I realized I had made a mistake. First, I didn't want to live with English speakers. Also, the sour-faced landlady would come over every day to "clean," which included sifting through our things in our bedrooms. Was this even legal? I wondered. I hated this woman from the start and I decided I needed to leave before I ended up karate-chopping this bitch in the throat and getting arrested in a foreign country. There was no way I was going to be hovered over like a child. I had already escaped the firm clutches of my mother and was an unencumbered young woman looking to make delicious mistakes.

I roamed the city, once more looking for a new place to live. This was before smartphones, so I relied on a paper (!) map and often had no idea where I was going. I would arrive to my appointments all sweaty and flustered. I considered one apartment with three men in their twenties, one of whom was a mouth-breather and seemed way too eager to rent me the room. I imagined a year of fending off his sticky advances and said no thanks. Another apartment I checked out was in the gay neighborhood, Chueca. It was dark and had no windows. The room I would rent was in the attic and the tenant made it clear that the rest of the space was his. He was a lugubrious fellow, and though I don't think he was interested in me sexually, something about him gave me the willies. There were many dead ends, and I was beginning to worry. I was in another country with no idea what I was doing. I feared I'd end up in a flophouse.

Then I found my apartment in Lavapiés, the immigrant neighborhood just south of the city center. I loved the humility of the name—the act of washing feet. My dour Spanish roommate from my first apartment had warned me about it, said it was dangerous, but once I stepped outside the Metro, I was in love: the fruit stores, the butcher shops, women in saris, people yelling in languages I couldn't recognize. It was so vibrant and noisy and the air smelled of meat and spices. This was where I was meant to be.

I rented a room from a Spanish woman in her early thirties who had short curly red hair and a friendly spirit. The apartment was tiny but bright and happy in a funky bohemian kind of way— plants, photographs of foreign places, and lively exotic prints. It was located in the interior of the building, a setup I had never seen before. All of the windows faced the courtyard or another side of the building. We got very little sunlight. My bedroom had a window that let in some light but looked onto a white wall. The kitchenette was so minuscule that we had to eat our meals hunched over the coffee table in the living room. At times it felt claustrophobic, but I still loved living there. I often heard neighbors across the courtyard arguing in Arabic and other languages I couldn't decipher. It all felt so multicultural and cosmopolitan.

There were no dryers, so everyone in the building hung their laundry on clotheslines outside their windows, and I eventually stopped being shy about my panties and let them fly freely in the wind for all to see.

Most of the immigrants in the neighborhood were young men, which was not surprising to me. I come from a family of immigrants, so I knew that often the men leave first and the women later follow. It's common for groups of Mexican men to live crammed together in small apartments while they send large chunks of their meager paychecks back home.

The streets of Lavapiés were always covered in dog shit. It was so ubiquitous it felt like part of the aesthetic. Though I never found it to be a menacing place, it was indeed a gritty neighborhood. It was dirty and populated with many homeless people and Spanish hipsters with ratty mullets and harem pants, which were in vogue at the time. (My friend Judy called them "cagalones," or "shit pants.") Sometimes I encountered the same three-legged dog that always looked hungry. I wasn't sure if it was a stray or someone's neglected pet. I felt sorry for the creature, but it seemed to have an optimistic attitude as it hobbled down the street. There was a woman with curly hair who wore a fake fur coat. I once saw her sitting on a bench with a little bit of blood dripping from her forehead, and now, almost twenty years later, I still feel a coil of guilt in my stomach for not asking her if she was OK. How could I have just walked past her like that?

There was the little person who cheerfully sold lottery tickets in front of the grocery store; the Romani women with their long skirts; and young African men all gathered in the square. There were a smattering of art galleries, one of which had a painting of a vagina dentata displayed in the window. Bars welcomed both dogs and children. There was so much to see it was almost dizzying, and my eyes were always greedy.

One of my favorite places in my neighborhood, and in the city, was Café Barbieri, a dimly lit place with tarnished mirrors and worn upholstery. I liked to sit there and write in my journal while drinking bitter coffee, because it made me feel like Ernest Hemingway—though I wasn't a misogynist asshole.

Cafés like this were alluring to me in Madrid. I have always loved old places and things. Spaces that are shiny and new make me a bit nervous; there is a certain expectation that they express, and I'm afraid I will disappoint. When a place has history, however, I like to think that I'm adding to it with my presence and that my body is occupying a space where so much has already happened—somewhere people have loved, cried, laughed, and experienced profound joys and disappointments. It's comforting to belong to an endless chain of stories.

Lavapiés had so much charisma and provided constant inspiration for my writing. I was in perpetual awe, always searching for something strange and beautiful. My responsibilities as a teaching assistant were minimal, so my evenings and weekends, and also Fridays, were free. Not to mention the daily siestas and the innumerable religious holidays. I spent so much time loafing that there were moments when guilt crept over me. How was I here on a bench people-watching in Spain while my parents were working in factories?

The Museo del Prado and Museo Reina Sofía were both within walking distance of my apartment, so I would spend many afternoons there luxuriating in the art and taking notes. I remember the moment I first saw *The Garden of Earthly Delights*, by Hieronymus Bosch. I had studied the painting in college and now here it was before me. I was giddy. People copulating! Strange mythical creatures! Naked figures gorging on ripe fruits! Birds pecking at stuff!

Was it greed, though? Or was it, like the title suggested, simply delight? Was it judgment? A celebration of being human? Regardless, I thought it was beautiful and it filled me with a lush wonder.

When I didn't have plans with friends, which was often, I'd roam the city gawking at people, exploring shops, peering into windows, drinking coffee, writing in my journal, reading books, eating tapas, and simply daydreaming. The aimless days let my imagination stretch in all directions. It wasn't until years later that I understood what a rare gift this was, particularly for a woman. The gift of solitude with few responsibilities. My life was mine and mine alone.

My first friend was a woman named Judy, a Jewish girl from Pennsylvania who had also received the Fulbright. She immediately made me cackle when she made a joke about MacGyver. We often traveled together and got into ridiculous situations. We were always pissing off bus drivers when we'd run onto the bus late as hell. We went dancing with all kinds of odd people. And once we got swindled by a person we assumed was a drug dealer. We deserved it for racially profiling him like that. When I think of that year I often think of Judy. Man, we would go out and party until some ungodly hour then go back to her apartment, where we would eat toasted ham sandwiches in her bed and fall asleep in our party clothes. In the morning I'd ride the train back to my neighborhood, looking disheveled in my crumpled jean jacket, feeling like someone had scooped my brain out.

There were many cultural events throughout the city that were free or affordable. Every Thursday I'd buy the city's leisure guide and circle all the events I wanted to attend.

Judy and I watched an Edward Albee play in which a man literally fell in love with a goat, which was as hilarious as it was horrifying. We held each other as the curtains fell. I saw a theatrical adaptation of *The Metamorphosis* that haunted me for days. I watched artsy movies by myself at the theater. I went to a modern dance performance in which they filled the stage with water and dancers elegantly rippled through it.

I also traveled to other cities to explore their art scenes. In Barcelona the architecture of Antoni Gaudí left me speechless. At the Guggenheim in Bilbao, Jenny Holzer LED signs flashed messages about the AIDS crisis: "I say your name," "I keep your clothes." In Paris I nearly lost my fucking mind at the Louvre. I couldn't conceive of the magnitude and the opulence. So many of the world's most iconic pieces all housed in the same space . . . it was surreal. When I saw Manet's *Olympia* at Musée d'Orsay, a painting I had seen in art books and adored, I could hardly believe my life. In Amsterdam, hallucinating on mushrooms, I stood in front of van Gogh's *Almond Blossoms* and my chest hurt because it was so beautiful. On spring break my roommate and I traveled to Morocco to a village painted almost entirely blue. At night we gathered in a café near the river, where young people sang and played the laud.

I was always bewildered. And I cried everywhere. A lot. It was not always the sad kind of crying, though. Sometimes it was a deluge of unidentifiable feelings that came out through my eyes.

The poetry of Federico García Lorca was one of the reasons Spain was so alluring to me. I didn't read his lecture on duende until years later, but I had an innate idea of what it was. All I knew is that Lorca's poetry gripped me by the throat.

I know I experienced duende when watching flamenco dancing. I couldn't tell you what it was, but I could see it, feel it in my organs. I loved the anguished look on the dancers' faces, the elegant stomping. It looked as if the music were killing them, and in that proximity to death they were most alive.

I found that the less conventionally attractive the dancers were, the greater their talent, and I didn't think this was a coincidence. Pretty, of course, is a privilege, and those who don't possess what the world deems desirable don't have the luxury of depending on their looks.

It was as if some of them were purging themselves of a spiritual malaise, as if they were casting out all their demons. The women weren't pretty, but they were beautiful.

In his lecture on duende, Lorca states: "We have said that the *duende* loves the edge, the wound, and draws close to places where forms fuse in a yearning beyond visible expression." The wound never heals. To me these women were dancing on that metaphorical blade, and now, many years later, they remind me of a myth I once read about a girl who danced until she couldn't stop, until her feet bled. Maybe she, too, was trying to heal the wound that never heals. Maybe that's what we're all doing. Maybe that's what it means to be alive.

I BEGAN TAKING a poetry class at a local literary organization, which turned out to be one of the best decisions of my life. Every Thursday night I would take the train to meet my class in a small conference room downtown. Our teacher, Jesus, was a big fat dude who always wore silly hats and smoked unfiltered cigarettes in class. He was funny and brilliant and gave us the most bizarre writing exercises to awaken our subconscious. One of them was a prompt in which we had to write the word "lamp" on a sheet of paper and place it on our bed as we slept. When we awakened, we were to write whatever came to mind without letting our rational selves get in the way. The poem I wrote in response to this exercise was about the man who consumed my thoughts that year. Part of it came to me as I walked alone one night. I stopped in the middle of the street to write an image of lucid semen trailing down a white sheet.

There were so many moments like these. I found inspiration at every turn, and there were times I could hardly stand it.

My class built a camaraderie I had always dreamt about. After each session, most of us would head to a nearby bar to drink beer, eat tapas, and continue our discussions about poetry. I loved these nights. We were all so different—a Goth girl, a teenager, a businessman in his forties, a posh woman in her twenties exploring her angst. And then there was María, "the one with the difficult name," who was my favorite of the group, and who years later became one of the most important feminist writers in the country. I was known as the American, or La Gringa, as they affectionately called me. I was the one who wrote the poem about a lynx eating her own young.

I had always been a loner, and at last I had found my people.

I WAS AN ILL-BEHAVED CHILD, which I'm sure is a surprise to no one. I often got low marks on "exercises self-control" because neither my mind nor my ass could ever keep still. Not surprisingly, I'm also a terrible planner. When traveling, I always have a handful of goals and no real agenda. All I want to do is eat, get lost, and people-watch. Rigid schedules depress me. This is why I've never been able to hold down a regular-person job without spiraling into misery. I prefer to be surprised, to show up to a place with few expectations and see where the day takes me. Sometimes I have an idea come to me as I'm performing a mundane task and I have to stop what I'm doing to write it down. I'm easily distracted and my moods can be unpredictable. The world is not built for people with this kind of temperament. Throughout my life, I've struggled to keep a semblance of normalcy so I can make a living and simply exist, but my mind is often a swirl of daydreams.

In *A Field Guide to Getting Lost*, a memoir by Rebecca Solnit, she describes the pleasure of submitting to the unknown. Of Virginia Woolf, she writes: "For [her], getting lost was not a matter of geography so much as identity, a passionate desire, even an urgent need, to become no one and anyone, to shake off the shackles that remind you who you are, who others think you are." This desire to abandon the self—perhaps, more accurately, the ego—is also why I love poetry and other forms of art. I want to bask in what I don't understand.

I have felt a kinship with Virginia Woolf ever since I read *Mrs. Dalloway* in my freshman English class when I was fourteen. The restlessness that the protagonist embodied felt so familiar to me. After finishing the book, I watched the film *The Hours*, based on the book by Michael Cunningham. I adored the movie, particularly the scene in which Woolf lies on the ground to stare at a dead bird. (I can't count how many times in my life a dead bird has made me lose my marbles.) In *A Room of One's Own*, Woolf wrote, "The beauty of the world . . . has two edges, one of laughter, one of anguish, cutting the heart asunder." She, too, recognized duende, so much that she walked into a river and drowned herself.

MY TEACHING ASSISTANTSHIP was at a junior high in a nearby suburb, a commute that involved two trains and a hell of a walk. I soon realized that I didn't love teaching. The kids were out of control and they didn't like me or my accent. How did I know? They told me. They were used to British English and believed the American version was inferior. One of them said that it sounded as if I were speaking with something in my mouth. He never specified what, but I used my deductive reasoning skills, because I am smart! I did the work because it was my job, but I didn't enjoy it. It was obvious they didn't respect me, and I often felt like a curiosity.

For the most part, I refused to speak Castilian Spanish during my year in Madrid. Sometimes I did adjust my diction for the sake of clarity, but as I mentioned previously, I was determined to be true to my Mexican identity. I never used the "vosotros" form, for instance. I insisted on "tu" and "usted," figuring that everyone would understand me just fine. They mostly did, but some took offense to my formal use of "usted" when referring to them. I did it out of respect, particularly for strangers, authority figures, and those who were significantly older than I was, but to some, it felt like I was being distant and unfriendly.

Some of the other Americans I knew spoke with the Spanish accent and lisp. I tried my best to avoid it, but it was inevitable that it would seep into my speech at some point. Once, on the phone with my mother, I heard myself say "grathias" instead of "gracias," and I was mortified. I hoped that she hadn't heard because I felt like a fucking prig. My mom is a humble woman, and I didn't want her to think I was putting on airs.

People sometimes ask me if I experienced racism while I was in Spain, and the answer is complicated. My racial ambiguity allowed me to blend in most of the time. I'm a light to medium brown, depending on the season, and most Spaniards didn't know what to make of me. Some strangers spoke to me in Arabic and I had to kindly let them know I didn't speak their language. Sometimes the locals laughed at my Spanish as if I were some sort of yokel. When I explained that I was Mexican American, Spaniards were often perplexed. How could I be both? they wondered. And why did I have a strange accent? I had trouble understanding what was so hard to understand. What I wanted to say was, "Your people savagely colonized the New World, thus birthing mestizos in the land that became Mexico; then, hundreds of years later, thanks to neoliberalism and corruption, these Mexicans, searching for work, immigrated to the United States, where they are exploited for their labor and treated like animals. I am the daughter of these immigrants, which is why my accent is not entirely Mexican. I struggled my way through college and now here I am on a fancy scholarship."

I belonged nowhere and everywhere all at once. I still live in this contradiction. I think we forget that people are composed of multitudes, contain many selves. I was never fully Mexican or American, and in Spain I was even more disoriented, so, in a sense, I became my own home. Virginia Woolf once said: "As a woman I have no country. As a woman I want no country. As a woman my country is the whole world."

When you don't belong, you learn to make a nest in the unknown.

SOMETIMES I WONDER who we would be without the conquest of the New World. I likely wouldn't exist, or perhaps a version of me would. What would our culture look like? How would women fare in a place like this? Sometimes I'm so angry at what feels like unending misogyny, and I want to point the finger at someone, but the truth is that what has led us here is a very complicated tapestry of hate. That's why I try not to romanticize Indigenous civilizations in this context or any. There are some who like to pretend that pre-Colombian times were the halcyon days. I once got into a futile argument with a Mexican man who insisted that machismo was imported from Spain, as if all the native women of the New

World were living in some sort of feminist utopia. I don't deny that the Old World's version of patriarchy was imported to the colonies, but I don't think we should fool ourselves into thinking anyone, especially women, was better off. There are times I morbidly wonder how many women were raped for me to exist. According to one anthropologist, the typical Aztec man expected his woman to be "tied to her *metate*, the *comal*, and the preparation of the tortilla." The women existed to make babies, serve men, and pass down their culture and traditions. Men valued virginity, were polygamists, and often had concubines. I find it delusional to think that Europeans—or anyone, for that matter—have a monopoly on misogyny.

IT'S FUNNY TO ME to think back on how much of a feminist I believed myself to be while simultaneously being someone's side piece. I believed Abdul loved me in his own fucked-up way, and he called me nearly every day, but he was still married and emotionally abusive. I had a hell of a time reconciling all that. I guess it's more accurate to say that I repressed a lot of my conflicting feelings. I was so desperate to be seen, to be loved, to be acknowledged, that I would have done anything to keep whatever semblance of those things our relationship gave me. It was like an illness—one that too many women succumb to. I allowed Abdul to manipulate me until I was so twisted and confused I couldn't reason. One day I was the love of his life, the next day he wanted nothing to do with me. It was an endless and excruciating back-and-forth that I felt like I couldn't escape.

I can blame him for all that happened, but it wouldn't be fair or accurate. Yes, he was older; yes, he was a man and therefore more powerful; but I had so many opportunities to leave him—I was halfway across the world, for fuck's sake—and I chose not to. I chose to stay. I had agency and chose my own oppression. But is it that much of a choice considering the life I had lived? I was basically a child, and who had ever taught me how to love myself? I live with that tangle of truths.

For months, I obsessed about Abdul's prospective visit. I hadn't seen him since September, and the plan was that he'd visit sometime in January. As the date approached, both of us worried he wouldn't be granted a visitor's visa because the world was so anti-Muslim at the time (still is!). It was 2007, in the thick of the Iraq War, and 9/11 was still fresh. We were both elated when he was given permission to travel, and at the start of the New Year, he told his wife some lie about visiting his family in Britain and came to see me in Madrid.

I thought I would burst out of my skin that week; none of it felt real. All the longing I had nursed those few months was at last being satiated. To be in the same place at the same time felt like a hallucination.

The day after he arrived we took a bus to Granada to see the Alhambra. Our timing was bad and the palace was on the verge of closing, so we could only race through the immaculate lawns and magical courtyards. The sun was about to set and the light was perfect. We took tacky pictures of us kissing. We held hands and looked into each other's eyes.

We left for Córdoba the next morning. I got motion sickness on the bus, and after we got off, I thought I might throw up. I expected Abdul to coddle me and treat me like a fragile little princess, but instead he lit a cigarette, which only worsened my nausea. I told him so, and he pretended not to hear me.

I purloined an orange from one of the ubiquitous orange trees. I gnawed on it in the hotel room, disappointed to find it so sour it was almost inedible. I later learned that the oranges were decorative, never meant to be eaten. What a strange notion. Everything on that trip happened so quickly that all the memories are jumbled together in my head, though I do remember that in an attempt to be romantic, Abdul hired a horse-drawn carriage to take us back to the bus station to return to Madrid.

He brought me a bloodred sari with silver embroidery from Chicago. It was one of the most beautiful pieces of clothing I've ever owned, and I still lament losing it in one of my many moves, even though the silver had begun to tarnish. We had plans to dress up for a nice dinner on one of his last nights in Madrid, but neither one of us had any idea how to wrap the sari. We looked online and still couldn't figure it out, so Abdul suggested that we go out into my neighborhood and try to find an Indian woman. I didn't have any better ideas, so we walked the streets hoping to spot a woman who looked like she could help me get dressed.

After roaming Lavapiés for a while, we went inside a fruit store. Abdul spoke to the owner in Urdu, and a few minutes later, his wife materialized and ushered me into a cramped and dirty back room, where she tied the sari for me. We laughed at the silliness of it all.

Right before he left, Abdul and I walked down Calle de la

Montera. He decided to stop at a pay phone to check on his son. He couldn't call from my apartment in case my number showed up on the caller ID. I stepped away to make it seem like I was giving him privacy, but I was trying to listen to every word. They spoke in Urdu, so I had to rely on his tone. As I waited, a man circled me, assuming that I was a sex worker.

At the end of the phone call Abdul laughed. At what, I'll never know. I never asked.

A FEW WEEKS AFTER ABDUL LEFT, as I returned to Madrid from a trip to Salamanca with friends, I received a text message from him saying that he never wanted to see me again. After his visit, this was too much for me to take. Something had finally shattered inside me. It turned out to be his wife who had actually sent the text, which only made matters worse. Abdul said that she'd taken his phone. He apologized over and over, but this time I couldn't forgive him. I was eviscerated.

Sometimes instead of getting lost for the sake of freedom, to escape my own ego, I wanted to annihilate myself—to get lost in someone else, to get lost in pleasure, to disappear because the act of living was too painful. I wanted to leave my body and enter someone else. I wanted to be so saturated with the presence of another that I vanished, even if it was fleeting.

NEXT CAME THE Mexican man who was fifteen years older and asked me to lend him money. I got rid of him real fast because I didn't hate myself *that* much. Then came the two Mohammeds. The first was my butcher, a Moroccan man in his late twenties. I flirted with him as he handled my meat, which sounds like a joke, but is the literal truth. He usually had cuts on his hands and arms, which now makes me realize he probably wasn't the best butcher. The playful banter—mostly him saying God knows what in his broken Spanish and me giggling—went on for weeks until one afternoon I saw him out in the street and suggested he take me out that night.

We went to a dance club that evening and then headed back to my place. We had sex, and for the first time in my dumb life, the condom broke. I honestly thought that was a myth. I was *aghast*, borderline hysterical, and kicked him out of my apartment. I obsessed and obsessed for two days until I realized I should get the morning-after pill before I ended up pregnant. After some research, I headed to a clinic downtown, where a kind woman gave me a prescription even though, I learned upon arriving, I was too old to be there—the clinic was meant for people under twenty. The pill made me nauseated. I wandered the streets that evening and evaluated my shitty life choices with hot tears in my eyes.

Mohammed and I continued to see each other for a few weeks. He spoke very broken Spanish, and I didn't speak a lick of Arabic, so communication was difficult. I don't even know if we had anything in common. Most of the time we just had sex and laughed at our inability to have a conversation.

I met the other Mohammed at my friend María's birthday party. His pickup line was, "Are you the Mexican girl?" He was Tunisian but spoke perfect Spanish, so perfect that he had the linguistic skills to be hilarious. He even had a PhD in Spanish literature. I envied this because my Spanish was still not polished enough for me to be as funny as I wanted; I often floundered in my jokes as I translated them in my head.

That night we shared a bus to the city center. I was headed to Paris the following day, so we couldn't meet for another week.

The night after I returned from my trip, Mohammed and I went to a flamenco bar in the city. It was in a beautiful and crowded underground space filled with candles and wooden fixtures. The music was amazing and the sexual tension between us was unmistakable. At one point during the performance, we both turned to look at each other and began to kiss. We couldn't stop. The music, the ambiance, the anticipation made it all so intoxicating. We left quickly after, as we couldn't keep our hands off each other. We didn't have sex that night because I didn't want him to think I was slutty. I liked him—he was funny and handsome in an understated kind of way. I dumped the butcher soon after, but I'll admit there was a bit of an overlap.

After about three weeks, I bestowed upon Mohammed the gift of my sex. After very brief intercourse, however, he was unable to get another erection. What I mean is that, save one time, we were not physically able to have penis-in-vagina sex again. He had some deep insecurities and anxieties that I could not even begin to comprehend. Each time we tried he grew exasperated.

This went on for several weeks, until I returned home to Chicago. It was spring and I was scheduled to leave July 1. Sometimes I wonder why I kept dating a person who was unable to meet my most basic needs. In a sense, I used one body to replace another. I was so desperate for his affection that I planned a romantic trip to Sevilla before I left. In my naive imagination, I believed that the setting would make everything better. That if we were in a different place, perhaps he could relax and we could properly consummate the relationship—a relationship that, without sex, was so utterly confusing.

Of course that didn't work. The trip was a disaster and ended with us in the hotel room drunk out of our minds. I tried to seduce him, but again, nothing. I stood at the foot of the bed in my lacy black underwear, face streaked with tears and makeup, and yelled, "This should be enough!" as I pointed to my body. Looking back, I wish I'd understood then that his impotence had nothing to do with me. It was not my proudest moment, and of course, my outburst only made things worse.

THERE'S ALWAYS BEEN a part of me that is vast and empty. Though I have a vivid inner life and find so much meaning in books, art, writing, and relationships, there's something deep inside me that feels like an insatiable pit. No matter the circumstances, there's never enough. Maybe that's one way to describe my depression: a bottomless desire for which I will destroy everything in my path in a fruitless attempt to satisfy.

Beauty in its various forms is what makes me feel most complete—a poem that obliterates me, a painting that makes me gasp, a song that fills me with inexplicable wonder. But once that passes, it's there again: the absence, the void, the need, the gaping hole of nothingness. I've tried to fill it with everything I could: sex, men, cigarettes, alcohol, travel, food, and generally living reck-lessly, often harming my body in the process, but these salves were only temporary. These salves were not salves at all.

The night before I left, I had a big dinner with my classmates, roommate, and all the friends I had made during my year in Ma-drid. My poetry class made me a poster with sweet and silly mes-sages. I realized I was loved.

We spilled out into the streets after dinner. It was Pride week-end and the city was brimming with people. At times I panicked, but I was excited by the energy of it all. It was what I had been looking for when I arrived: bright lights, exuberance, friendship, poetry. We staggered through the city and danced. I didn't want it to end.

THAT MORNING I sobbed as I waited for my plane, already nostal-gic and so hungover I felt like a meat vessel full of mild poison. The woman next to me asked if I was OK, wondered what was wrong. When I didn't have a good answer, she became upset. "I thought someone had died," she scolded me and turned around. But how could I explain any of it to her? That I didn't want to leave a place that had given me so much. That I had traveled here to escape myself, my drudgery, and my suffering, only to find them at every turn.

LA MALA VIDA

My umbilical cord almost strangled me when I was born. In some of my darker moments, I joke that I was a suicidal fetus. This is not entirely hyperbolic, considering how much time I've spent depressed during the thirty-seven years of my existence. I've always had a flair for the dramatic.

But I was strange well before birth. While seven months pregnant, my mother says she heard me cry in her womb. She sat in our old living room as my brother—five at the time—played with his toys on the ugly brown carpet. I twisted inside her and she rubbed her belly to calm me. It was brief, she said, but unmistakable: I cried. She then reassured me everything was fine, that she was excited to see me soon, and that I was loved.

And so I stopped.

Shortly after, my mother told one of her coworkers about the incident. According to this coworker, babies who cry in utero are supposed to be geniuses or have some sort of gift. I wouldn't call myself a genius, but I always knew that I was different, my sensitivity so acute, I felt as if I walked through the world with flayed skin.

My mom says that my melancholy took over her, too. She had never been as emotional as when she was pregnant with me. Everything made her cry. People couldn't even look at her without her bursting into tears. I hurt her before I even arrived.

"COMO TE GUSTA LA MALA VIDA," my mom has often said to me throughout my life. I suspect many other Brown girls hear the same admonishment from their families. My mother believed that I always chose the darkest, thorniest path when there was a perfectly pristine road available to me. But "a girl gets sick of a rose," you feel me? Though I rolled my eyes at the time, she was right. I did make my life much more complicated than it needed to be. I sought drama and searched for obstacles, both consciously and unconsciously. I was bored by normalcy and stability. Perhaps this is one of the reasons I became a writer—a poet, specifically. All signs point to a life of poverty, obscurity, and unnecessary strife? Well then, please sign me up. I'm forever exhilarated by high stakes, the possibility of failing monumentally.

MY MOM LIKES to tell a story of me at the age of two that is a sort of foreboding of my recklessness. My family was outside my grandparents' house in Mexico, and I was left unattended for no more than a few moments. By the time they turned to me, I was already climbing the ladder that leaned against the house, more than halfway to the roof. Everyone was stunned, afraid I'd plummet to my death. "¡Cuerpo sin alma!" my grandfather yelled. In retrospect, this description is accurate, because I always felt that my soul, or whatever it was, didn't fit inside my body. I felt too much. I didn't work right.

In the end I was rescued intact. With shaky legs, my mom climbed the ladder and carried me down.

On this same trip, my mom had a premonition one night as I was sleeping. Bothered by a vague worry, she lifted the pillow beneath my head and discovered a centipede. I've always remembered it as a scorpion, however, because sometimes we remember the version we prefer. Of her three children, I have always given my mom the most trouble, and I believe the trip was a harbinger for the pain in the ass I would become.

In *One Hundred Years of Solitude,* Gabriel García Márquez wrote of human beings that they "are not born once and for all on the day their mothers give birth to them, but that life obliges them over and over again to give birth to themselves." This reminds me of the Frida Kahlo painting *My Birth,* in which her adult head is coming out of her own vagina. In her journal she writes that she is giving birth to herself in the painting. This is also how I perceive my self-birth: brutal, bloody, and grotesque.

MY MOM REGULARLY attended a Saturday night "círculo de oración," a prayer group in the Little Village neighborhood of Chicago. Mexican immigrants would gather to discuss their challenges and receive emotional and spiritual support from one another. I hated attending but I didn't have a choice in the matter, because I was seven. My mother would drag me there every few weeks and I would sit in the pew bored out of my mind, waiting for it to end. In retrospect, it was a beautiful communion of oppressed people, but I was too young and depressed to see that at the time. One night I had what my mom called "la chiripiorca," a temper tantrum from the aforementioned classic Mexican TV show *Chespirito*. I started crying for some mysterious reason and she was unable to calm me down. She kept asking me what was wrong, but I was inconsolable and didn't know how to articulate what was happening to me. I don't remember what brought this on, but I'm certain that I didn't want to be there. I hated church, and sadness would creep up on me like a thick fog whenever I was there. I was already prone to depressive bouts, and anything church-related just exacerbated them. That night, everyone gathered around to pray for me, but that didn't help. I remained distraught. My mom had to take me home.

I BECAME AN ATHEIST at the age of twelve, when I realized the Catholic Church hated women. There was so much that didn't make sense to me. Why couldn't women be priests? How was Eve made of a man's rib? And what were all those sermons about obeying our fathers and husbands? All my questions remained unanswered.

I stopped believing in God altogether because there was no reasonable explanation for suffering, including my own. Why did everything hurt so much? Why were African children starving to death in commercials during Christmas? Why did men rape? Why did it feel like my heart was always splitting open like a fallen fruit?

My older brother, having mastered the art of duplicity, learned to go through the motions and pretend to believe for the sake of peace. I, on the other hand, could never keep my mouth shut. I wanted to be *understood*. I wanted to be seen for who I was. The easiest method would have been to nod, smile, and go along with my parents' worldview, but as my mom repeatedly pointed out, I liked to make my life harder. I've always been bad at faking things. Though I often lied to my parents about my whereabouts, I couldn't lie about something so important.

Despite my incessant protests, my mother threatened me with punishment and dragged me to church. Every Sunday morning I'd sit through a never-ending mass, my head darting around like a confused bird's. I studied the fellow parishioners to entertain myself and stay awake. I most delighted in funny haircuts and ugly outfits, of which there were plenty. I studied the saints with their rolled-back eyes in the stained glass windows. I wondered about the lambs and the men in heavy brown robes holding wooden staffs. What did it all mean? And what did it have to do with me? I traced Christ's jutting ribs as he hung from the cross and cringed at the tone-deaf choir. Something about it all scared me, but I wasn't sure what.

Catholicism felt like a bag of jagged rocks tied to my feet.

I don't think it's a coincidence that I discovered poetry at about this time. I was searching for an escape, a place to be myself, to be free in a world in which I didn't belong. We read Edgar Allan Poe in my sixth-grade class, and I became entranced by the music, dark imagery, and sense of alienation in his poems. A quiet ferocity bloomed within me and I decided that poetry was what I was meant to do. I would often introduce myself as "a poet." The audacity makes me laugh now. No es por nada, but I was a bold little fucker.

My depression always made happiness a fickle and fleeting son of a bitch. It didn't have a name or shape then, was something I couldn't understand or articulate. A container for my grief. All I knew was that there was a sadness that hovered over me like a sticky cloud, made it hard to live. I was able to pinpoint specific moments when I believed I was happy, but it never lasted for extended periods of time. I found most of my solace in reading, writing, and music. Happiness was abnormal, something worthy of applause and celebration. If I was in a good mood for longer than a few hours, it was almost astonishing. I was angry at being alive, at having to exist in human form. I wanted to disappear. I began thinking of suicide when I was about thirteen. Sometimes I'd take my busted boom box into the bathroom to drown out the sound of my crying as I showered.

As a child, I always lived in the future, my mind perpetually imagining the older version of me—traveling, writing, and doing as I pleased. I found the present dull and oppressive, and the future embodied a boundless freedom. My interior world has always been sacred to me, and I could spend all of my days attempting to describe it. Maybe that's what all my writing is—the failure to describe the ineffable. I have dedicated my entire life to this failure.

When I was eight, my mom, older brother, and I took a trip to Los Angeles to visit relatives, our first vacation besides our summer road trips to Mexico. One afternoon, my uncle drove us to Malibu, and as I stood on the beach in my bathing suit watching the gargantuan waves, something overwhelmed me. The sight was almost too beautiful to take in. I felt the expanse of the universe in my body and it made me tremble.

I had my first psychiatric hospitalization at the age of fifteen. Shortly after, I traveled to Mexico with my best friend Claudia and her family. One afternoon, we rode bikes into the country and stopped to rest in the shade. Next to me there was a puddle of mud that reflected in the most delicate and beautiful way, and I just sat there looking at it in disbelief.

I always knew I was spiritually deficient. It was not quite poverty—I had a rich inner life—but it was definitely a malnourishment I was choosing not to address. Early in my life I decided that Catholicism wasn't for me, but I still yearned for something to help guide my life. My depression was so often debilitating, and I wondered if there was a way to make sense of it. Could there be something that could possibly ameliorate the pain I always carried? Poetry was the closest thing I had to religion, and although I loved it with every fiber of my being, I still felt disconnected to the world, irrelevant, even, and that restlessness always managed to gnaw away at me.

In Buddhism this discomfort is called *kha*, which means "sky," "ether," or "hole." In her book *The Faraway Nearby*, Rebecca Solnit explains this word can be translated as "discord or disturbance, the antithesis of harmony or serenity." The concept of attachment in Buddhist philosophy is one of the main causes of suffering. As human beings, we cling to things that are temporary, which often hurts us. Buddhists believe that if we came to terms with the impermanent nature of life, appreciated the present moment, and let go of the desires that cause us harm, we could lead happier lives. I had always wanted so much, so this idea illuminated much of my misery. I believe that art and transformation often come from this friction between desire and attainment, the attempt to fill an absence. We attempt to make meaning of our human experience. We have to.

Though I wrote about my suffering in poetry, I wondered if my existential malaise could be solved with a spiritual practice. I had already concluded that Christianity was harmful to me; I couldn't come to terms with the explicit oppression, but I believed there was something beyond me that I didn't understand—a force or energy that ruled the world and would explain everything.

I bought a book on meditation (maybe I stole it, I don't remember), but I failed at it, or so I believed. I sat on the floor of my cramped bedroom one night and tried to wipe my brain of any thoughts. I imagined the ocean or sky, but my mind was spastic and unyielding and I quickly grew frustrated and gave up. I've always had a short attention span, my ideas climbing on top of each other. How was it possible to think of nothing at all? What kind of wizardry was this?

I decided I didn't care for material things during this phase. I shaved off all my hair (please note this was the early aughts, before it was mainstream) and bought hideous clothing from thrift stores that didn't fit right. I fantasized about running from our consumerist society to a remote monastery and living there forever. I held on to this rather inaccurate and romantic idea of Buddhism for a long time—me in an orange robe alone on a mountaintop.

Though I quickly abandoned meditation, something about the Buddhist faith pulled at me for years. I didn't quite know what the practice involved, but I believed that Buddhists were more serene and aware than the rest of us. I was also aware that the Buddha himself was a teacher rather than a god, which appealed to me, because I never liked the idea of groveling. Getting on my knees to beg a manlike entity for forgiveness? Get the fuck out of here.

I began reading Walt Whitman's *Leaves of Grass* and was intrigued by his belief in pantheism, the idea that the universe is the manifestation of God and that reality and divinity are one and the same. The notion that we are all sacred. I never understood why the Catholic faith insisted that we were filthy inside.

I loved Whitman's sprawling lines and lush language. On my way home from school one day, I read the poem "There Was a Child Went Forth." It was spring and the snow was thawing at last. That was my favorite time of year—the end of winter, when the world smells like wet dirt and the birds begin to return. I cried as I read the poem. Like the boy, I often felt like I was made of everything I saw and touched. "The early lilacs became part of this child, / and grass and white and red morning-glories, and the white and red clover, and the song of the phoebe-bird." The poem made me wistful, euphoric.

I was also comforted by Whitman's line from another poem in *Song of Myself*: "look for me under your boot-soles." To me, the idea of one day becoming dirt that will nourish flowers and trees illustrates the humility and transcendence of the human body.

For all these moments of interconnectedness, I had many existential freak-outs. Sometimes I was completely tranquil, and then all of a sudden I'd be grazed by melancholy, which would then turn into an internal catastrophe. At times like these, nothing had any meaning and everything inside me ached. The world pulsed with an unbearable stillness. Time stretched on like a terrible honey.

The first time I read *Nausea*, by Jean-Paul Sartre, I was both devastated and comforted by the protagonist's bleak view of himself and everything around him. As he studies his face in the mirror he wonders, "Do other men have as much difficulty in appraising their face?" It's the same question I've had for most of my life.

In my midtwenties, I was desperate for some spiritual relief when I was working at a marketing company in the Sears Tower. I would often cry in the office bathroom or as I walked home from the train. The culture was in direct opposition to who I was, and I felt like I was being tested like a character in a Greek myth. I think I may have preferred an eternity of birds pecking at my liver to wearing business casual and pretending to give a shit about alcohol advertisements.

I knew I was depressed, but I hadn't seen a therapist since grad school two years prior, and I completely stopped taking medication during my first year of college, five years before that. None of the antidepressants I took ever made me feel level, so I had written them off altogether. One medication made me so numb that I would stare blankly at everything, which was in some ways more frightening than anguish. Pain I knew, but I had no idea what to do with indifference.

It was at this time that a Tibetan Buddhist temple opened in my hometown, of all places. It made no sense to me because Cicero is a predominantly Mexican working-class town, and I would venture to guess that nearly every resident is Catholic. The center was only a few blocks away from my childhood home, where my parents still live to this day, and it felt like an omen.

That the temple was located in a former art store seemed to further suggest how out of place it was. How many poor Mexicans were in the market for oil paintings? How did that place even stay open for that long? I hadn't visited that store since I was a teenager, and even then, it was owing to how much I'd always loved art and was generally captivated by the building's unusual architecture. The place was dark, musty, cramped, and brimming with drab old paintings. Now I was back in the building as a grown woman in search of spiritual guidance.

I was greeted by a blue-eyed man with a thick southern accent who talked about himself incessantly, which was puzzling, as one of the tenets of Buddhism is releasing the ego. He gave me a tour and explained that the building was once a speakeasy with a secret door, which added to the mystique of the place. I soon met other members, most of whom were cliquish and not at all interested in me or my religious quest. Weren't Buddhists supposed to be nice?

Still, I attended Sunday services for a while, hoping something would suddenly click into place and it would all make sense. I didn't know any of the chants and spent my first service thinking of the delicious bacon-fried beans I had eaten the night before. I don't know why, but this ridiculous craving took over me. This was not really what I had in mind, daydreaming about saturated fats. *I'm doing it wrong*, I thought to myself. I stopped attending soon after, when a young man there began sexually harassing me. A tale as old as time!

About four years later, on the cusp of a monumental nervous breakdown, I was invited to an international literature and free speech festival in Stavanger, Norway. I never in my life imagined that I'd travel to Scandinavia, but here I was with four other writers from Chicago, gorging on pickled fish for breakfast and discussing the role of art in political resistance.

One of my fellow writers there, Jackson, is hilarious, brash, and completely sure of themself, a person with an infectious spirit. Jackson is Black and trans, and despite all the forms of abuse they've endured from the world, they are so present and alive. I was drawn to them immediately, and I knew that we'd be friends. We talked about race and sex with an openness I always crave in friendships. I wanted Jackson's joy and self-confidence. I liked the way they laughed with their whole body. When they told me they practiced Buddhism, it made perfect sense to me.

Our Chicago group met exiled writers from several war-torn countries. Manal, a poet from Iraq, had left her country with her son after her husband was killed for political reasons. She wrote stark love poems that reminded me of the Nordic landscape. A young Afghan translator told the story of fleeing his country and walking to Greece after the Taliban had killed his little brother for working with American soldiers.

Some of the writers didn't speak about what had happened to them, but the trauma was palpable. Together, they made a tiny community, despite living in remote places of that cold and unfamiliar country.

The Norwegians were polite, but not warm. This, I thought, was evidenced by their muted colors and the eerie absence of laughter in the streets. Everyone was so measured, and it made me, an impulsive and animated person, uncomfortable. I felt like a macaw with my loud laugh and bright clothing.

Though I didn't feel embraced by the land, Norway was indeed beautiful and transformative. One of the most memorable parts of our stay was a trip to the fjords. For most of the tour, I stood at the front of the ship and let the wind whip my hair into tangles. The air smelled incredible. I had that feeling again—a oneness with my surroundings and a deep inner calm. As I watched the mountains and waterfalls, the only thing that came to mind was the word "sublime." I felt lucky to be alive and I wanted to hold on to that forever.

UPON RETURNING FROM NORWAY, I continued to descend into my depression. No one knew that I often thought about killing myself and almost drove myself to a psychiatric hospital on several occasions. Jackson invited me to Buddhist meetings; they belonged to a lay organization that promotes peace through Nichiren Buddhism. I always had some excuse for why I couldn't go—I was too tired; it was snowing; I had to write; blah, blah, blah. But eventually I managed to drag myself out of my apartment and attend a gathering downtown with them.

I've always considered myself to be open-minded, but I'll admit

I was suspicious when I arrived at the meeting. I heard the rhythmic chanting as I approached the door and was greeted by smiling faces. Everyone was so friendly and welcoming that it made me nervous. There was an exuberance I had never witnessed before and I found it unsettling. How was it possible to be so happy? What kind of pill had these people swallowed? Now I look back, embarrassed for myself. Why did I consider kindness an anomaly? Was I really so fucked up at this point in my life that genuine joy frightened me? I was skeptical but intrigued by the practice nonetheless. In theory, I wanted to learn more about the philosophy, but there were times I couldn't get out of the fetal position. I tried chanting, which felt more tangible than meditation, but I still wasn't grasping it. I felt self-conscious and sometimes even stupid.

That winter, Jackson moved to Los Angeles, and if it weren't for their friend Andy, who inevitably became my friend, too, I probably would have given up. Andy gently prodded me to attend meetings despite how frequently I flaked out. It was as if someone were handing me an elixir to save my life, and I kept smacking it out of their hands. While Prozac, therapy, and quitting my very stressful public relations job helped me crawl out of my depression, I knew I was still lacking something on a fundamental level.

Several months after my first meeting, after many stops, starts, and doubts, I converted officially, which included receiving a scroll and an object of devotion, and setting up my altar. I had never trusted happiness, but I was determined to learn how.

To believe that a higher being has my life in its clutches is not only absurd but sadistic to me. What kind of God, for instance, would give me debilitating depression and willingly bestow humankind with genocide, pediatric cancer, and Donald Trump? Why would anyone want to believe in such a cruel being? That is not the kind of God I would ever want to believe in. He sounds like a dick.

Buddhism, by contrast, asked me to believe in the law of cause and effect, something that can be proven by science. Karma, which is the spiritual principle of the practice, therefore, makes perfect sense to me. Many people mistakenly believe that karma is reaping what you've sown, or getting what you deserve. I wish that were the case. (If that were true, Donald Trump would be living in a trash heap for the rest of his life with a multitude of parasites feasting upon him, and even then, it would take eons for him to pay for what he's done.) "Karma" literally means "action," and it contains the power and results within our actions. In Buddhism, there is no heaven and hell where people are rewarded or punished for how they've lived. Buddhism holds that what you do, whether it's good or bad, has consequences, even if we don't see them in our lifetime. Those consequences can be delayed and manifest themselves in complicated ways.

Another tenet of Buddhism that spoke to me is the interrelatedness of all things, which is a concept I already believed from my many years of writing and studying poetry. So instead of imposing an absolute doctrine, Buddhism asked me to consider how my actions might affect others.

I found this much more comforting than the notion of some sort of cruel puppeteer in the sky who fucks with the universe according to his whims. My life as an accumulation of causes before, during, and after my existence? Well, that I can deal with. Through this new lens, I began to see the way that I often created my own unhappiness. As Nichiren Buddha wrote, "Misfortune comes from one's mouth and ruins one."

I see my own life as a transformation of the karma I inherited. I was born into a family of immigrants and laborers. The women who came before me were impoverished and had little agency. They endured hardships and abuse that I can't even comprehend. Instead of perpetuating this cycle, I decided that this wouldn't be my fate. I didn't choose my circumstances, but I chose how I would react to them. And though I know that part of this was my personal responsibility, I'm also aware of the privileges I have: I'm an American citizen, I was born in a time and place less hostile toward women, I'm able-bodied, I'm mostly straight, I'm relatively light-skinned, I had access to an education. However, I'm still a Brown woman in America. This shit is not easy. I hope that in changing many of my circumstances I create better conditions for my children.

MEDIEVAL FEMALE MYSTICS would mortify themselves to get closer to God. When I first read about them, I was fascinated with the esoteric practice—punishing the body for its sinful nature, extinguishing all that is earthly. I was particularly fascinated by their hair shirts and other self-flagellating tools, like rods and whips. Why would anyone choose to live this way? Suffering in this case wasn't an inevitable by-product of being alive; it was a willful act, a production. That sort of martyrdom has always bothered me to my very core, because, goddamn it, isn't it hard enough to be a woman? But maybe even that was better than being married to a man. Still, I was angry at these mystics. I often witnessed this in Mexican culture—the spectacle of pain in telenovelas and the veneration of self-sacrificing mothers, to name a few examples. It frustrated me when my own mother tried to manipulate me with guilt, because I never asked her to suffer on my behalf. I never asked Christ to die for my sins either.

There is a poem titled "Emptying Town," by the poet and memoirist Nick Flynn, whose ending illustrates this, and it always knocks the wind out of me: "My version of hell / is someone ripping open his shirt / and saying, Look what I did for you . . ."

SOME PEOPLE HAVE judged me for taking antidepressants, as if being suicidal is more noble than being medicated. A boyfriend I had in high school once urged me to abandon my medication and "suffer like a warrior." But why should I invite pain when so much of it is inescapable?

A few years ago, I came across an essay about Mother Teresa in *Vanity Fair* written by the late Christopher Hitchens. Hitchens accuses the saint of voluntarily inflicting pain on people who were already downtrodden. And he argues, here and elsewhere, that she was a fraud:

> MT [*Mother Teresa*] was not a friend of the poor. She
> was a friend of *poverty*. She said that suffering was a gift
> from God. She spent her life opposing the only known
> cure for poverty, which is the empowerment of women

and the emancipation of them from a livestock version of compulsory reproduction.

Though I have often disagreed with Hitchens, I have to give him props for calling out Mother Teresa's hypocrisy. He points out that while she ran decrepit hospices in Calcutta, she herself received the best medical care in California clinics.

An Indian doctor similarly claimed that she created "a cult of suffering," and that her clinics were so primitive that they reused hypodermic needles and patients were forced to defecate in front of one another. If the doctor's word is to be believed, this kind of suffering cannot be considered noble. It is manufactured and therefore perverse. Who could it possibly benefit? God? If so, *how*, exactly? We can't but believe that Mother Teresa used her position in the Church to impose pain in the name of religion. And she was glorified for it.

In most cases, I find martyrdom of the self-flagellating variety to be repugnant; I have, however, considered that for some women, self-flagellating may be an opportunity to wield power in the only way that is available to them. It is the epitome of passive aggression and almost brilliant in a sense.

THERE'S A STORY about the founder of the faith, Shakyamuni Buddha, that begins with him meditating at the foot of a mucalinda tree after reaching enlightenment. When it begins to pour, a giant king cobra comes out, coils its body seven times around the Buddha to keep him warm, and places its hood over his head to protect him from the rain.

This story is beautiful to me because I never considered something being at once so dangerous and yet also capable of protecting us. In her book *When Things Fall Apart*, Buddhist monk Pema Chödrön puts this idea into perspective: "What we habitually regard as obstacles are not really our enemies, but rather our friends." It may be that what we fear has the most to teach us. Buddhist philosophy began to teach me to embrace my pain, to hold it with tenderness and compassion, to accept it as one of the many facets of being human. It takes death for there to be rebirth.

A FRIEND OF mine once commented that he'd never heard anyone say that "la buena vida" had really inspired them or that they'd learned so much from it. I agreed. Happiness is wonderful, but it is not in itself interesting. Who wants to read a book in which the protagonist gets everything she wants exactly when she wants it? But the fucked-up road to happiness? Now, that deserves its own elaborate stage. I've been able to sit with discomfort through poetry, which I'm beginning to see as inextricably linked to Buddhism. In writing poems about the ambiguity and hurt of being alive, I was already practicing the philosophy.

Some of my fellow Buddhists had promised that my whole life would change, but I wasn't prepared for a metamorphosis. For so long I had come to terms with living with depression; I believed there was only so much I could do to alleviate that existential pain.

It was who I was. I knew I'd never be fully cured of my mental illness, but I found a sense of determination that I never knew I was capable of. In *Hope in the Dark*, Rebecca Solnit writes that "to hope is to give yourself to the future." Hope is brave.

Although I always had many dreams and aspirations, much of my life was about enduring, or aguantando—I just wanted to make it through without falling apart. I never considered that I might be capable of a more trusting outlook. I had never given myself permission, because I didn't know that I was allowed. I have a framed picture of Sartre with the quote "Hell is other people," which I bought while I was in Paris. It has followed me to many apartments, and for years, I sincerely believed its message to be true. I was misanthropic, and whenever I had a conflict in a relationship, I was quick to point fingers. *It couldn't possibly be me*, I often thought, because I was introspective and therefore self-aware. In Buddhism, hell is not an afterlife full of fire and scratchy clothing. It's a miserable life state in the present, one that I was very familiar with. It wasn't until I began to truly look inward that I realized I was wrong about the source of conflict in my relationships—the inferno wasn't other people; *I* was my own inferno.

ACCORDING TO BUDDHIST THOUGHT, our inner lives contain ten worlds: hell, hunger, animality, anger, humanity, rapture, learning, realization, bodhisattva, and Buddhahood. The first six are considered the six lower worlds, and in Nichiren Buddhism, these are not stationary conditions. Instead, we acknowledge that the worlds are fluid and we are capable of inhabiting them all at once. We contain multitudes, as Walt Whitman once declared. Even in our most hateful moments, the potential for Buddhahood still lies within us. In a world that prefers binaries and absolutes, there is something so reassuring about that.

I knew, in theory, that my environment mirrored my inner state—I learned that when I began to study—but it soon became achingly clear.

THE JAPANESE ART of kintsugi involves repairing broken pottery with lacquer mixed with gold, silver, or platinum dust. Wabi-sabi is an aesthetic concept based on the idea of imperfection and transience. In this philosophy, breakage and repair are part of the object's narrative rather than a mistake that needs to be cloaked. The brokenness is what makes it more beautiful. When I learned about this tradition, I thought of the ways I had shattered months before. I had spent so much of my life coping, and it wasn't until I truly, *epically* fell apart that I was able to construct myself into the person I always wanted to be.

It's hard to explain what happened next. As I recuperated from my depression and developed a strong spiritual foundation, I became kinder, my friendships deepened, and my career flourished. I was in control of my life for what felt like the first time. The law of cause and effect, which in retrospect seems like such an obvious concept, finally clicked in my brain. Though I was here because of who and what came before, I created my reality with the choices I made. As I chanted, I began to see unhealthy patterns and found the courage to dismantle them. I was confronted with myself, like someone had handed me a mirror, and I was startled to see my own face. For so long I didn't like parts of who I was but felt incapable of changing them. I would just study these unsavory personality traits with no clue of how to proceed. I often got on my own nerves.

It's no coincidence that my first marriage ended during this time. While chanting one afternoon, I stared at a stone with the word "clarity" carved into it—a gift from a friend—and I became aware that I had never been loved the way I needed to be loved, that there was no way to save my eight-year relationship. We had been married for a little over a year and we were already imploding. I think we needed to go all in to realize we needed to end.

I began to plan my departure as soon as I realized I needed to be alone. I didn't blame my husband, though. That would have been too simple and unfair. I saw all the ways in which I was complicit. I learned how I participated in my own suffering. If I didn't believe that I myself was sacred, why would anyone else? If I didn't believe I was worthy of a deep and boundless love, why would anyone give it to me?

My whole life I had learned to accept scraps of affection and attention. It's what I thought I deserved. This explained why all my romantic relationships have been dysfunctional, why I pined for men who had so little to give me.

I USED TO believe that happiness would arrive when my problems disappeared. What I didn't understand was that they never would. I hadn't come to terms with the inevitability of obstacles. If only I had more money. If only my career were in a better place. If only people wouldn't hurt me. If only men weren't such trash. In my mind, happiness was a magical land devoid of conflict. I didn't know the difference between relative and absolute happiness. The former is always dependent on outside circumstances. Happiness was a rarity because everything in my life had to align perfectly for me to experience it. Absolute happiness, on the other hand, is indestructible. Even in our most dismal moments, we're capable of joy. We can use our suffering to deepen the meaning of our lives.

Though I was in some ways devastated by the disintegration of my marriage, I was excited to begin again. I had always known, deep down, that we weren't meant for each other. We were so incompatible, but I had convinced myself that I could make it work by repressing all my needs and desires. It was the practice of Buddhism that helped me see that I had been lying to myself for many years. This kind of realization, in retrospect, is not at all surprising because chanting is often described as polishing a mirror. I was finally able to see myself.

A THIRD-CENTURY BUDDHIST philosopher named Nagarjuna once compared the Lotus Sutra, the highest teaching for Nichiren Buddhists, to "a great physician who can change poison into medicine." That is a guiding principle that always brings me comfort. Instead of bemoaning my misfortune, I learned to ask myself what I was going to do about it. Yes, I had grappled with depression my whole life, and yes, it was unfair, but what was I going to do with that experience? And yes, my marriage was ending a year and a half in, but what was I going to learn from it? I could resent my circumstances or turn them into something meaningful. This process, this act of birthing, is called "human revolution," a term I love because it implies personal responsibility to transform the self; by changing who we are, we change the world around us.

I had been so accustomed to fixating on the past and future that my new appreciation for the here and now felt extraordinary. I didn't have to fantasize about being elsewhere anymore. As a result, I began to feel immense gratitude for everyday objects and experiences. When I saw something beautiful as I was running through the city—a rusted bridge, an unusual flower in a parking lot, an airplane cutting the sky with its exhaust—I stopped and literally said thank you. I made sure to do it aloud because it felt more meaningful to acknowledge it with my voice. I thanked the universe for the fact that I exist, which at times felt like a miracle, and that I had the privilege of witnessing a particular form of beauty at that exact moment. How many organisms had to evolve for me to simply be me? I wondered. When I thought of this, sometimes it scared me, the vastness of it all, the improbability of it all.

All the moments of transcendence I've experienced throughout my life, those times when everything shimmers and I am in complete communion with my environment, finally had an explanation. In Buddhist philosophy the principle of three thousand realms in a single moment of life described why I felt limitless. All the "innumerable phenomena of the universe . . . encompassed in a single moment in a common mortal's life." Our bodies are temporary, but we are boundless. The truth is eternal and karma lives on forever. With this in mind, neither life nor death scared me any longer. Our lives are not limited to the present, but stretch beyond anything we can ever imagine. The macrocosm is contained in the microcosm. Every person is a universe. This is why I wrote poetry. This is why I've always been suspicious of borders, why I prefer in-between places, why I'm more interested in questions than in answers. I had always been Buddhist. I just didn't know it.

I USED TO worry that my desires were too strong. Sometimes I wanted things with such unbridled desperation that it scared me. I ached with it. It's not that I wanted objects, though—I've never been materialistic. I wanted knowledge, agency, and beauty. I wanted to be recognized for my talents and live a rich and interesting life guided by art and social justice. I wondered if it was possible to be Buddhist when I felt this way.

I learned that the point was not to eradicate desires, but to cultivate them based on compassion and wisdom. Nichiren Buddhism acknowledges that desires are part of the human experience. We all want love, after all. And the quest for enlightenment is itself a form of yearning. I had to remind myself that I was not motivated by greed. I wasn't seeking riches or world domination. I wasn't trying to build my happiness on the misfortune of others. In fact, I wanted to make the world a better place with my work. I realized that it wasn't about not wanting, but rather, knowing how to want.

IN COLLEGE I read Ntozake Shange's *For Colored Girls Who Have Considered Suicide/When the Rainbow Is Enuf,* and one of the lines in the book cracked me all the way open. It articulated what I had been striving for: "i found god in myself / and i loved her / i loved her fiercely." I wanted so much to believe this statement, but it would be many more years until I had the wisdom to do so.

As a woman, I found Buddhism liberating and empowering. I didn't have to revere a man or subjugate myself in any form. It wasn't a faith powered by shame or guilt. I was not a wretch, sinner, whore, or supplicant. I was a whole person, a flawed and loving person. I learned to see myself with compassion, to acknowledge Buddhahood or "God" in myself and others. Instead of beseeching a savior, I relied on myself.

I think this is the reason that I so often write about the violence people inflict upon one another. So much of my poetry explores this confusion. If human beings are all capable of being compassionate and just, what happens to a person to make them abandon their humanity? And where do we go from there?

SOMETIMES WHEN I think of Shakyamuni leaving his palace of riches and comfort to seek the truth by any means necessary—including extreme asceticism and self-mortification—I think of my mother's admonishment: "Como te gusta la mala vida." As a prince, as Siddhartha Gautama, he had everything a person could ever dream of, and yet he renounced it to understand the nature of suffering in order to liberate humankind from the bondage of ignorance. Rebecca Solnit beautifully describes this journey as "a fairy tale run backward."

Well into his spiritual practice, the Buddha fasted for so long that it's believed he could touch his spine through his belly. After this he meditated under the bodhi tree and had a revelation. Siddhartha Gautama transformed into the Buddha when he perceived himself as one with the universe. He *was* the universe.

The Buddha also discovered that suffering—through sickness, old age, and death—was inevitable. Life is impermanent and we experience anguish when we fight against this fact. The only way to alleviate that pain is to come to terms with it, respond to it with wisdom. Buddhism asks you to believe in yourself and use your unique gifts to make the world a better place. Though it sounds like an incredibly obvious concept, it's taken me my entire adult life to believe and internalize it. Sometimes the simplest things are the most elusive. When I let these truths into my heart, I finally surrendered my doubt and understood that I always belonged on this earth, that I was always eternal.

I can't possibly compare my life to that of the Buddha, but I also chose discomfort over complacency. By becoming a poet, by living on my own terms, by leaving my marriage. I couldn't keep lying to myself. I preferred to live my truth, no matter how uncomfortable that was. I knew I was making room for an extraordinary love.

DO YOU THINK I'M PRETTY?
CIRCLE YES OR NO

When I was four years old, I climbed atop our bathroom sink to look in the mirror and determine if I was ugly. My uncle had just remarked, "Ay mija, cómo estás fea," and I didn't understand that he'd meant it affectionately, that in fact he'd meant the opposite. That's just the way Mexicans show love.

I had my hair in a tight French braid, which was typical throughout my childhood and often caused me headaches. Like many Mexican mothers, mine would twist and pull my heavy brown hair into intricate designs and styles. There is so much pride Mexican women take in the appearance of their children.

I stood on the sink and stared at my big nose and thick lips, transfixed by my own face, and wondered if my uncle was right. As I debated the question of my beauty, my mother walked into the bathroom and burst out laughing. She knew exactly what I was doing and reassured me that I was, in fact, pretty, and that my uncle was only teasing me.

My family often reminisces about my confusion that day.

"Remember when you thought you were ugly?" We laugh because of course I wasn't! Still, I wondered about this throughout my young life. Did the world think I was ugly? What did it mean to be pretty? Who got to decide? I didn't know many in real life, but it seemed that little white girls were always lavished with so much attention on TV. *They must be the pretty ones*, I thought.

PUBERTY WAS A particularly painful time for me. I assume this is the case for most girls. As soon as I turned twelve, I became sweaty and chubby in all the wrong places. It was as if my body had betrayed me. No one had prepared me for this. I soon sprouted blackheads on my nose and a constellation of pimples on my forehead. When I look back at pictures of those years, I feel a combination of pity and amusement. My favorite is a cheap portrait of me in front of a baby-blue backdrop. I was wearing one of my most beloved shirts—a polyester tie-dye number with giant lapels covered in garish colors and flowers that looked like they were exploding. This, paired with fitted Levi's and brown leather platforms, was one of my go-to outfits. I find this adorable because holy shit I looked terrible. I had taken my gigantic glasses off for the picture and my face was all squinty and splotchy. My smile was tentative, so awkward it looked like a smug grimace. My shoulder-length hair was poorly cut, as if someone had put it in a ponytail and chopped it off with a cleaver—the work of the cheap salons on Cermak Road, where señoras would give me twelve-dollar haircuts that were outdated by at least a decade.

For years, I wanted to hide under a rock, ashamed of simply

existing and having a physical body. I hated looking in the mirror. I wanted so much to be pretty, but I was uncomfortable with every aspect of my being and had no idea how to even begin to do anything about it. All of my pathetic little crushes were unrequited. No one—and I mean *no one*—ever liked me. I didn't look like the popular girls at school with their heavy makeup, big boobs, and cool sneakers. And I certainly didn't resemble the skinny white girls in the '90s sitcoms I loved—*Full House, Saved by the Bell, Sabrina the Teenage Witch*. For one, I was the wrong color. The lightest of light browns was still too brown. When I watched *Beverly Hills, 90210*, I was so confused that Donna Martin, played by Tori Spelling, was considered a hot girl. To me, she looked like a sad horse in desperate need of a torta. Were all blond women automatically considered beautiful? Was I missing something? Was this some kind of conspiracy?

Meanwhile, it was always alarming when someone was skinny in my family. It meant they were sick or malnourished. *Ay dios ¿estará empachada?* It's hard to translate "empacho," and there's no consensus on what it means, but it's generally understood to suggest that something funky is going on with your stomach that has made you lose your appetite. Some people believe it means "constipated" or "disgusted." Also, poor people—of the Mexican variety, at least—may think you suffer from lombrices, parasites. In fact, a common and hilarious insult for someone who is thin is "lombriciento," which literally means "filled with worms."

I was confused—TV said that I was chubby, while thinness was a cause for concern among my people. What was the ideal weight, then? I had no clue. Further adding to my confusion, when I was about eleven years old, my maternal grandmother shamed me about my appetite. I was hell-bent on eating a foot-long submarine sandwich one afternoon and trying to convince my cousin who was visiting from out of town to join me. My sandwich journey would take us a few blocks down to a magical place called Mr. Submarine (yes, I am mentioning it again), and my cousin seemed all but convinced when my grandmother quipped, "Por eso estás como estás." I just stood there stunned.

My body was a disappointment to everyone.

I tried throwing up once after I ate, like I had seen in a made-for-TV movie, but I was so disgusted as I looked at the flecks of bright vomit in the toilet that I never did it again. Besides, it seemed like such a waste of food.

I'VE BEEN CONFUSED FOR GREEK, Italian, Middle Eastern, Indian, and all kinds of Latin American. On very rare occasions, to my chagrin, people even think I'm some kind of white. This seems silly to me given my big nose and lips, but alas. ("My name is *Sánchez*," I tell them frantically. "*Sánchez!*") My skin is a light to medium brown, the color of a very milky coffee, not quite caramel, with strong yellow undertones. I can't wear any shade of orange or yellow without looking diseased. (At school, many girls of my complexion insisted on being blondes, which I found to be aesthetically jarring.) I once wore a blond wig for Halloween (David Bowie in *Labyrinth*), and though I rocked it, I also looked jaundiced. My nose is large and slightly upturned. A man I once dated described it as "proud." The faint bump on the bridge gives it an aquiline quality, one that I likely inherited from my Indigenous ancestors.

My lips are probably the most noticeable thing about me. Really, my face is half mouth. During an interview once, a photographer asked me to smile less for my portrait, which made me laugh. My ex-husband told me he didn't like making out with me because my mouth was "too big" and it felt like it was engulfing his face. (Strangely, his was the first and only complaint I ever received about that.) I have also been blessed with beautiful Mexican hair. It's medium brown and people often comment on how thick and shiny it is, and I'm embarrassed to admit how much I enjoy these compliments. After all, I didn't do anything to deserve it. "Una bendición de pelo," my mother used to say as she brushed it into a tight ponytail.

My light brown color and my relatively slim and able body allow me the privilege of blending into many spaces. I know I'm able to move through the world in ways that other people of color are not. My presence isn't always questioned and my body isn't automatically feared.

I TAUGHT IN the Dominican Republic during my semester abroad when I was nineteen, and some of the girls I taught—their skin all manner of brown with hair very nearly black—these girls would draw pictures of themselves with blue eyes and blond hair. I wonder where they are now and if they still think their skin is the color of peaches. Strangely enough, they reminded me of my maternal grandmother. With brown skin and thick, dark braids, she looks undeniably Indigenous, and yet it was she who told my little brother that his next girlfriend should be tall and blond, and then was appalled when my mother asked her how she would react if he fell in love with a Black woman. I wonder what she sees when she looks in the mirror. Does she have some sort of dysmorphia? Does colonialism reach that deep into her psyche?

Among much of my family, being dark is undesirable. Some relatives use the word "indio" as a slur against darker-skinned Mexicans. The word "prieto," which means "dark complexioned," can be either affectionate or derogatory, depending on the context and tone, and it is used liberally. A family member once praised the Spanish for "bettering" our race.

COLORISM AND ANTI-BLACKNESS in Mexican culture has a long history rooted in colonialism. Mexico had a very complicated legal caste system in the 1700s. To exert control over their colonies, the Spanish commissioned paintings to illustrate different racial distinctions. As the cultural historian John Charles Chasteen describes in his book *Born in Blood and Fire*, a person's caste was recorded in their baptismal register, and those of lower (and darker-skinned) castes were legally barred from, among other things, becoming priests, owning weapons, attending university, and even wearing silk. There were sixteen theoretical categories in all, but only six were typically used. Some of the lower castes were derisively given animal names such as Wolf or Coyote. Although the members of the six categories were legally prohibited from mixing, there was, of course, a whole lot of boinking and raping going on, so mixing was inevitable. Interestingly, the Spanish crown was desperate for money, so they allowed successful members from the lower castes to purchase exemptions. You could actually buy your whiteness. I wonder how many people today would line up for that shit. I can imagine Latinx Trump supporters coming out in droves. Assholes.

WHAT ALWAYS EXASPERATES me about the colorism and racism in Mexican culture, particularly in the United States, is the sheer foolishness of it. I want to scream, *White people don't like us either, you dummies.* In fact, vilifying the undocumented, especially Mexicans, is a central component of Americans' self-mythologizing. But this is the nature of colonialism and white supremacy—oppressed people are pitted against each other in order to keep the power structures intact.

In *Black Looks: Race and Representation*, bell hooks explains: "From slavery on, white supremacists have recognized that control over images is central to the maintenance of any system of racial domination." If we saw how much we had in common, we might collectively push against this system of white supremacy. Instead, we clamor over each other, desperately clawing for the approval of white culture. How easily some Mexicans forget that our Indigenous ancestors were also subjugated, enslaved, and decimated. How easily they forget that Mexico was also part of the transatlantic slave trade.

. . .

I'D LIKE TO THINK that I've always been above backward attitudes about race, but that wouldn't be true at all. I internalized the racism and colorism all around me and believed that whiteness was more beautiful. There were times when I was a kid that I considered how much easier life would be if I were white. Those girls on TV . . . their lives seemed so effortless. Then there were the Spanish-language shows always playing in the background. In the telenovelas the rich protagonists were always light-skinned, while the servants and evil-doers were dark with Indigenous features. The sexy women on the god-awful variety show *Sábado Gigante*, and even on news programs, were always voluptuous and fair. I felt like a straight-up goblin by comparison.

The summer I turned fourteen, I magically lost weight and grew boobs. It was disorienting at first to suddenly feel like I could stand to look in a mirror, but soon after, I began to feel that not only could I look in a mirror, but I might actually like what I saw. I began high school with a more curvaceous body and a stylish bob with bright red bangs. Though I was far from confident, I was a bit more comfortable with my appearance. I was, in some ways, growing into myself. But that came with consequences—men began to leer at me more hungrily than before. When classes let out, older men were always circling the block looking for young women. I couldn't go anywhere without getting honked at. Danger lurked everywhere.

Now I understand that all this attention had nothing to do with sexual desire. Those men would have ogled anything they suspected was female. After all, I had been catcalled since I was a shapeless eleven-year-old in baggy clothing. In *The Beauty Myth*, Naomi Wolf explains this dynamic: "Women are watched . . . not to make sure they will 'be good,' but to make sure they will know they are being watched."

I was just learning my place in the world.

WHEN YOU'RE A young woman, simply having a body is a hazard. I think of my paternal grandmother, Clara, who at the age of eleven, two years after her father was murdered, was stalked by one of his friends. This man, a widower, began coming around their family farm and told my grandmother that he wanted to take her as his wife. She was the same age as his daughter at the time. Of course, my grandmother refused, and then told him he should pray on it. When he threatened to take her by force, she became afraid. With her father gone, her family was perpetually vulnerable to outsiders, and she wasn't sure how to protect herself from him, especially when she was away from the family farm.

One evening, she and her younger brother saw the man approaching the property on horseback. Panicked, my grandmother found her father's old gun, a carbine that overpowered her small frame. She and her brother climbed to the roof of the house and decided that they would shoot him. They even considered where they would bury the body and what they'd do with the horse. As the man grew closer, my grandmother aimed her gun with the full intention of killing him. She took aim and fired, and the force of it knocked her back. When she got back up, she saw that she'd shot his hat off his head. Startled, the man fled on his horse and never returned.

When I hear accounts like this, or when men harass me, I think of the myth of Daphne. The story goes that because she was so beautiful, Daphne caught the attention of Apollo, who pursued her so relentlessly that, in her desperation to be rid of him, she pleaded with her father, Peneus, to save her. In response, he turned her into a laurel tree, and she remained this way forever. Even then, Apollo took her leaves and wore them on his head, which became a symbol of both Apollo and poetry. This poor girl turned into a goddamned tree to escape him, and the motherfucker *still* wouldn't leave her alone.

DURING MY FIRST two years of high school, I went through a disheveled Goth phase in which I dyed my hair jet-black and wore fishnets and combat boots. I found some leftover white Halloween makeup in my drawer from an old vampire costume and started to add it to my foundation. Though I wasn't conscious of all of the fucked-up history and implications around skin lightening, I thought lighter skin was more attractive. I liked the contrast of it against my black hair and believed that it made me look edgy and mysterious, when it actually made me look like a corpse. While attempting to lighten my skin remains one of the most shameful things I've ever done in my life, it's not entirely surprising that I tried it. The messaging was everywhere.

I read *Seventeen* magazine religiously, and it was filled with tips and tricks for how to ostensibly be white. One of their makeup techniques bid the reader to make her nose look smaller, and naturally, I went for it. It involved drawing a line of concealer down the length of my nose and subtly blending it in on the sides. This practice is now called "contouring." (To my disappointment, my nose did not look any smaller.) I was so embarrassed by my large mouth and lips at that time, if there'd been a tutorial for minimizing them, I would have tried it. The word "trompa," which means "trumpet," was commonly used to describe my mouth. My friends in high school also called me Chompers, for a time, and when I asked my kooky English teacher if I indeed had big teeth, he responded, "Yeah, you have beautiful horse teeth like my wife."

I didn't know whether to be flattered or insulted. I think I may have laughed.

My mother, who grew up in a shack in the middle of nowhere with no dentist or even real toothpaste, always reminds me how lucky I am to have straight, healthy teeth. Had they grown in crooked, she says, they would have remained crooked. During our summer trips to Mexico, I was always startled by the stark difference between teeth in the United States and teeth in Mexico. In Mexico, it was much more common to have poor dental health. So many people's teeth were stained brown or capped with silver or gold in the outdated dentistry of the region. It was so ordinary that it wasn't even worth mentioning. While dental health in the United States is (not surprisingly) better overall, there were plenty of people in my Chicago neighborhood with tragic mouths. There was a white girl in my first-grade class, for instance, whose teeth were rotten little nubs. Her name was Stephanie, and she was always eating candy. I didn't realize it at the time, but her mother—a shaky and emaciated woman—was addicted to crack.

Teeth can say so much. I was fascinated when I learned that ancient Mayans modified their teeth with grooves, notches, and semiprecious stones to make themselves more attractive. Perhaps the lower classes used silver and gold in their own attempt to signify prosperity. Or maybe it was just the cheapest way to do it. Who the hell knows?

GROWING UP, I was never comfortable with being noticed. I wanted people to acknowledge me for who I was, but no one could. In my junior year of high school, I went through an ascetic phase during which I donned thrift clothes that were on the verge of falling apart. One of my favorite dresses at the time was a bright orange number that had probably belonged to a Midwestern farm lady. All of my jeans were old and frayed, and I paired everything, even tattered skirts and dresses, with a pair of dorky red sneakers. I loved wearing used clothing because I liked to imagine the lives of the people who had once owned them.

After a bad haircut one evening, I took my dad's clippers and shaved off most of my hair. I felt a sense of relief, but everyone else—parents, classmates, strangers—were horrified at what I had done. *Why would you do such a thing?* people wanted to know. The truth was that I wasn't entirely sure at the time, but I did know that beauty felt like a burden to me. *I don't care*, I would say and shrug.

Part of me already perceived myself as ugly, so I committed to it, went all in. The pressure to be aesthetically pleasing was too much, so I rejected it altogether. Somehow that seemed easier to me. I was afraid of femininity. I thought it would make me soft, that I would be even more vulnerable to predatory men, who, it seemed, were everywhere. There wasn't a single street in my neighborhood that was free of their harassment. Men were on every block, catcalling at all hours, so that even the most casual errands required strategizing. I didn't want to be objectified any further. To look masculine, as I believe I was attempting to do, was not my true nature; it was a coping mechanism, a survival method. This is the same reason I developed resting bitch face. Some people perceive this phenomenon as some sort of curse, a misfortune. They miss the point, don't understand that it can be a weapon, a face carved from years of harassment and unwanted attention. I'm aware that I have it, and I don't apologize for it.

Now in my late thirties, I love indulging my feminine sensibilities. For too long, I not only feared them, I didn't think I deserved to feel pretty or beautiful. Growing up poor, there was a part of me that believed I didn't deserve to spend time or money on what seemed frivolous. I never saw my mother spend money on herself. I remember that she had one Mary Kay lipstick that she always wore to family parties. Even now when she buys herself something that could be considered unnecessary, she tries to give it away. I learned to deny myself pleasure also.

When you're a woman, everyone has an opinion about your appearance, whether you like it or not. If you spend too much time and effort on the way you look, you're often considered vapid, vain, and self-indulgent. (How many times have I heard men say they prefer a woman without makeup? No, you don't, shut the fuck up.) If people think you don't care enough about your looks, you may be labeled as homely, unkempt, or slovenly. Really, there is no winning, so why even try to get it right?

Getting close to death obviously changes you in profound ways. After surviving my most recent depressive episode, in 2018, I began to see the world and myself through a different lens. I started to care less and less about other people's opinions of me. It's not that I didn't care about how others felt, it's that I no longer felt beholden to people I didn't have actual relationships with. Who cares about what some asshole says about me on Twitter? Who cares if some tangential person doesn't like me? So what if some distant relative doesn't approve of my life choices? We get one dumb life and I'm going to live it how I want. I decided that if I lived with integrity, I didn't have to worry whether people liked me. It was freeing to rid myself of that kind of weight. And this made me more and more comfortable with myself physically. Of course I'm not completely free of the standards of beauty, but the white male gaze becomes more and more irrelevant the older I get. Bye, bitch.

I wear what makes me feel beautiful. How could I live my fleeting, improbable human life hating the vessel I came in?

Until several years ago, I used to think my lips were too big for lipstick, that wearing it made me look like a clown. I had internalized the notion that large lips were vulgar because only white women had ever been praised for them. I didn't want to draw attention to a feature I believed to be excessive, showy. Now I wear the brightest shades of lipstick every day to draw attention to one of my best features. I also love frilly dresses, getting my nails done, and having long shiny hair. After years and years of therapy, getting more comfortable with who I am as I get older, and my incessant feminist analysis of the world around me, I finally have the means and the confidence to luxuriate in my femininity. My closet is full of bright colors and patterns. Lots of animal prints and hand-embroidered pieces. Some days I want to drape myself in gold like an empress. I wear large hoops and other dangly colorful earrings. I love expensive perfume in elegant bottles. Occasionally, I also wear what I couldn't afford to buy as a teenager: leather jackets and Doc Martens. I have learned to feel empowered by my softness, my shimmer, and my motherfucking drip.

At thirty-seven I love my body—my light brown skin, my short frame, my asymmetrical breasts, my thick thighs, and my generous ass. As a woman with agency and finally in control of her body and sexuality, I no longer feel ashamed of my physical form. Too feminine? Not feminine enough? Who the fuck cares? How I feel is what's relevant.

PARADIGMS OF BEAUTY are neither innate nor arbitrary. As Naomi Wolf explains, standards of beauty are driven by politics that uphold male supremacy. "The beauty myth is not about beauty at all," she writes. "It is about men's institutions of power." Beauty standards are essentially about control, specifically controlling women's bodies and, consequently, our behavior. If women are consumed by the desire for physical perfection, they are more likely to fixate on meeting the standard and much less likely to challenge whence it came: the patriarchy.

MY ASCETIC PHASE as a teenager didn't last long. I wasn't cut out for such austerity. If I'm honest with myself, part of me was not brave enough to lose the capital that my physical appearance granted me. I was well aware of the privilege of being pretty. I liked it. Sometimes the benefits were subtle and unspoken, and sometimes they were so blatant that it was staggering. When my head was shaved, people were often cold and unfriendly. Men didn't scramble to open doors for me. Strangers were often confused about my gender and that made them uncomfortable. Sometimes people were openly hostile. I once went into a restaurant to order a slice of pizza, and the cashier laughed in my face.

I tried to extinguish the part of me that valued my appearance, but I was unable to. The world is kinder to you when you look the way it wants you to look. Countless studies have shown that attractive people earn more money. In my late twenties and early thirties, my regard for my own beauty was so outsize that I'd cry and hole myself up in my apartment for days at a time whenever I had bouts of severe acne. I couldn't stand being perceived as anything less than pretty. I still can't. I know that part of the privilege I hold is due in part to being a young and attractive woman. Part of me is ashamed, and another part of me accepts that this is a consequence of living in a world where a woman's worth is inextricably attached to her appearance. Maybe beauty can be a weapon. Maybe I'm a fool.

. . .

I'M NOT NAIVE enough to believe we can do away with beauty standards. We can't look at our extraordinary world and believe we aren't wired to be in awe of gorgeous things. Humans have always beautified themselves in some form or other. This desire feels innate and primordial. Every day my eyes are pulled toward something lovely—a striking face, a glistening clavicle, a sunset behind an abandoned building. As a writer, I can think about nothing else.

The essayist Elaine Scarry, in her book *On Beauty and Being Just*, suggests that the defining characteristic of beauty is that it replicates itself. "It makes us draw it, take photographs of it, or describe it to other people." Plato—and everyday life—seems to support this claim: "When the eye sees someone beautiful, the whole body wants to reproduce that person." This is where art comes from. What is a love poem if not a replication of the beloved?

I'm strengthened by beauty and devote my life to it through words. Beauty doesn't equal hot chicks on TV, as capitalism has tried to make us believe. Scarry points out the flawed logic that beauty is inherently burdensome: "Beauty is sometimes disparaged on the ground that it causes a contagion of imitation, as when a legion of people begin to style themselves after a particular movie starlet, but this is just an imperfect version of a deeply beneficent momentum toward replication."

Though the body positivity movement is challenging the way we view women's bodies, an overwhelming amount of media continues to perpetuate unrealistic proportions and features. By today's standard, for instance, we're supposed to have a giant ass, full, perky breasts, big lips, and a flat stomach. Cellulite is seen as some sort of genetic curse. It and various other body "imperfections" can now be brought to submission by the use of body makeup. We can't ride in a cab or even pump our gas without a screen in our face showing us what we're supposed to look like. When I see women of color with terribly bleached hair and lightened skin, it speaks to the obdurate nature of colonialism, of hundreds of years of racial inequality, and I can't help but think it looks grotesque.

But beauty in itself is not the problem. The problem is who we let decide what is beautiful.

WOMEN AREN'T SUPPOSED to admit they're attractive. It even feels a bit uncomfortable to admit here that I think I'm beautiful. We are conditioned to bond over our "flaws." I can't even count how many times I've been among a group of women griping about the way they look or shaming themselves for being fat. Most of the time I just smile awkwardly, not knowing what to say. It's expected that you participate, and if you don't, you become suspect. Your forbearance reads as conceit. Capitalism thrives on our insecurities. When we feel inadequate or unattractive, we're compelled to buy products to feel better.

The fact that I believed that my nose was too wide and my lips were too big is a direct result of what I saw in the media touted as attractive. It's absurd to me now because (white) people pay for their lips to look like mine. But society only considers those features special and beautiful on white women. Kylie Jenner has made a career of this.

. . .

IN THE '90S, the French performance artist ORLAN began pushing the boundaries of plastic surgery to prove that beauty cannot be constructed. In *The Reincarnation of Saint ORLAN*, she underwent nine cosmetic and reconstructive surgeries to look like the ideal beauty in Western art as depicted by male artists. The results from some of her surgeries include: the nose from the sculpture of the goddess Diana, the mouth of Francois Boucher's Europa, the forehead of da Vinci's Mona Lisa, and the chin of Botticelli's Venus.

Despite these procedures, or rather, *because* of these procedures, many journalists deemed ORLAN "ugly" and even "puglike." If you believe that she looks unattractive and disturbing, as I do, you've proven her point: that the "ideal" is possible only through a visible image and not a physical body. Her intention was never to make herself more beautiful, but to show the ways that beauty standards oppress women. Though I can't help but think plastic surgery in this instance is barbaric and somewhat repulsive, I'm fascinated by a woman bold enough to butcher her own face over and over again to convince us that beauty can be a fucking liar.

SEVERAL YEARS AGO, I took a DNA test to discover my ethnic makeup. Though I had a vague idea of what it might be, I didn't have much information, as our family records in Mexico are difficult to find and in some cases nonexistent. I've asked my grandparents a million questions about our ancestry, but the answers are always nebulous. What a privilege it is to know your own history.

When I saw my results, I ran around the room in a frenzy. "Holy shit!" I screamed. "This is the best day ever!" I could hardly contain myself. What I had wondered for so long was broken down into a simple pie chart. The test revealed how multifaceted I suspected I was. I'm significantly Spanish and Indigenous, of course, but I also have traces of other European as well as African ancestry. Suddenly, the way I looked made perfect sense to me.

I still have days when I look in the mirror and pick myself apart—the dark circles under my eyes, my oily skin, the pimple likely on my chin, the strong jawline I inherited from my father. But mostly, when I see myself, I understand something I didn't before: that I get to decide what is and isn't beautiful. There are moments I'm simply amazed that I have consciousness, that I'm alive. It almost feels like a miracle to be this person, to be me. There are times I see myself and see the whole world. I look at my face and see multitudes.

CRYING IN
THE BATHROOM

It was October 2014, and I had fallen into the worst depression of my life, the darkness outside enveloping me in a crippling and unfamiliar despair. My therapist asked if I ever thought about suicide. I said no, but the truth was that I thought about it several times a day. I'd rent a cabin in Michigan and off myself with a bottle of wine and a fistful of pills. I'd listen to the beautiful piano works of Erik Satie as I slipped out of consciousness and into a peaceful oblivion. I was never able to say it out loud.

At thirty, my life was in shambles. I'd escaped my childhood to pursue the dream of becoming a writer, and here I was, a grown woman, paralyzed with hopelessness and self-doubt. All I could do was binge-watch *Gilmore Girls*, finding a sliver of comfort in the idyllic New England town of Stars Hollow, the benign and quirky characters, and the silly capers they got into. I loved watching the interactions between Lorelei and her daughter, Rory, because they were so unlike my relationship with my own mother.

. . .

As soon as I hit puberty, my mother and I began to resent each other. Our relationship was nothing like the wholesome white fantasies I saw on TV. I grew up in a working-class Mexican neighborhood that was plagued with violence and squalor. Sex workers and their clients loitered in front of a seedy motel at the end of our block. Fun fact: the first penis I ever saw belonged to a man flashing a sex worker. My brother saw people literally having sex behind our building. Strange men snorted drugs off our garbage cans. Gangs were ubiquitous. Once, a man tore my mother's gold chain off her neck and then slapped my brother until he fell to the ground when he tried to protect her.

I struggled to find a place for myself in this environment. I had always been an unusual kid; most of my family and my peers misunderstood me, disliked me, or both. Most girls my age looked like traditional Mexican daughters with their neat clothes and braided hair. Others wore more urban clothes—sneakers, basketball jerseys, and large hoop earrings. Meanwhile, I wore combat boots, flappy black dresses, and band T-shirts. I dyed my short hair funny colors. When I "became a woman" and my sexuality began to flourish, I became a nuisance to my parents, particularly my mother. I had strong opinions that no one agreed with. I was a feminist, hated church, enjoyed solitude, and loved to read and write. I was always scandalizing my mother in some form or another. One of my earliest forms of rebellion was shaving my legs. I was thirteen and my dark hair was growing in thick as cactus spines. Embarrassed, I secretly used my dad's razor in the shower.

One afternoon we were at a family party at my uncle's house. It was summer and I was wearing a pair of overall shorts, and as I passed my mother sitting on the stairs, I felt her hand brush against my leg. "Hija de la chingada," she muttered, her face flushed with anger.

I constantly complained about the unfair distribution of labor in our house. Why did I have to heat tortillas for my brother? Didn't he have hands? Why couldn't it be the other way around? And how come the men always ate first even though the women did all the work? To my mother's chagrin, I was not at all interested in housework. Anytime she tried to teach me how to cook, it would end with me storming out of the kitchen, exasperated by her criticism and bored as hell by the minutiae of chopping onions, sorting beans, and frying tortillas.

My mother grew up in a wooden shack in rural Mexico. The daughter of a migrant worker in the Bracero Program in the United States and a frequently ill mother, she had to run the household and take care of her seven siblings. As the eldest daughter, she began cooking at the age of five, which might sound cute if the circumstances weren't so depressing. She made tortillas from scratch and by hand. She was smart and driven but was only allowed a few years of schooling in her remote mountain village. She still laments that she was only able to complete sixth grade. This resulted in a very narrow worldview, particularly when it came to gender norms. In 1978, at the age of twenty-one, she immigrated to the United States with my father. Two decades later, when her daughter began to act like an Americanized teenager, she was rightly bewildered, and reacted how any Catholic Mexican mom would—with unbridled control. She wanted to know my where-abouts at all times, grew suspicious of me whenever I left the house. Though she was only trying to protect me, she always suspected the worst and did everything in her power to prevent me from getting pregnant and ruining my life. A fear I now understand.

In the beginning, I just wanted room to breathe. After a while, though, I did in fact do the kinds of things she feared: I experimented with drugs, had sex, pierced body parts, and even got a shitty tattoo in some guy's gross attic. I'd try anything to quell my restlessness. Once I punched a door after an argument with my parents. Sometimes I cut myself.

To escape the bleakness of my environment and my tense relationship with my mother, I lost myself in books. I latched on to writing. Writing brought me joy. I excelled at it and hoped it would offer me a way out. I realize now that it was also convenient and inexpensive. All I needed was a pen and paper. I had many other interests—particularly art and music—but those required many more resources, money we didn't have. My parents once bought me an acoustic guitar at a garage sale, but I soon gave up when we couldn't afford lessons and I was unable to teach myself with library books. Writing was the cheapest way to feel free. I was scrutinized and controlled at home, and the blank page offered me endless possibilities, a vehicle to create another reality for myself.

In high school a few teachers noticed my talent and encouraged me to keep writing. Mr. Cislo, my freshman English teacher, was particularly supportive and would give me mixtapes and books he thought I'd like. Once he even made me a packet of all his favorite poetry. The work of Sharon Olds, Anne Sexton, and Sandra Cisneros—women who wrote unapologetically about their bodies and inner lives—opened up a vast space inside me. Writing felt like an emergency. And so I wrote poems about menstruation, sex, and sadness. And trees, of course. Always trees.

My sophomore year I got censored in our literary magazine for using the word "cunt." Another time I was reprimanded for reading a poem about my vagina at a school assembly. I was scandalous like that.

WHILE I WAS brooding in my room reading Anne Sexton and writing about my body, most of my family members were breaking their backs as laborers. My dad got up at dawn to make cheese-cakes with my uncles and cousins in a factory on the west side of Chicago. My mom worked the night shift at a paper factory and came home with cracked, chapped hands and melancholic eyes.

My aunt, who worked at a candy factory, looked at my hands when I was about thirteen and told me I had "manos de rica." It was true—they were smooth and soft rich-lady hands. On top of all the cooking and cleaning, the women in my family had jobs that involved intense manual labor. Every day my mother came home to never-ending housework. Who could blame her for being perpetually tired and irritable? Her life was full of hardship. Her world revolved around us and the factory, and there was little room for anything else. She never did anything for herself, never had the luxury of time or money, no hobbies or good friends to unwind with after work. When I was eight or so, I used her face cream thinking it was body lotion, and she was so angry and disappointed. Why? she wanted to know. Why would I do such a thing? At the time I had no idea why she was yelling at me over moisturizer, but now I understand that it was probably one of the few things she ever indulged in, and I had taken it from her.

Success in my family meant sitting at a desk; it meant you had air-conditioning during the brutal summer months; it meant your boss didn't talk down to you because you didn't speak English; it meant you didn't fear la migra would deport your ass while you were minding your own business trying to make a living.

Neither of my parents made it past sixth grade, so at thirteen, my brothers and I had already surpassed their level of education. My older brother and I became our parents' interpreters and cultural brokers. We translated legal documents and important medical information. The power dynamic between non-native-speaking immigrants and their American-born children can be mystifying for those who have never had to advocate for their disempowered parents. Sometimes we had to be the caretakers, whether we liked it or not. Talking to strangers and asking for things became easy for me. I learned to shed any sense of self-consciousness or intimidation, because my parents needed me—at a parent-teacher conference, at the mall, or on the phone with an insurance company.

When I was fifteen, my mom and I were at a diner, and as usual, I was in charge of communicating with the server. She scowled as she took our order and then turned around and chatted gleefully with the white people sitting next to us. Enraged, I wrote a note on a napkin: "Mexicans are people too." Such a simple phrase, it was not at all the bite that would become characteristic of my personality, but it felt brave to simply speak up, to assert myself and the personhood of my people. And indeed, being a mouthpiece for my parents taught me to be assertive. I learned to stand up for myself. I learned to get shit done.

People often ask me who my role models were growing up, and the truth is that that designation went solely to Lisa Simpson. To me, Lisa was brilliant and utterly unafraid to be who she was. I loved the way she earnestly voiced her unpopular opinions about all kinds of issues: feminism, literature, animal rights, immigration. Sure, she was sometimes irritating and overzealous, but damn, she had gumption and integrity. Lisa was just about everything I wanted to be, and I related to her in ways that I didn't even understand at the time. I saw myself in her when she sabotaged Homer's barbecue by destroying his roasted pig in her quest to save the animals of the world. That's exactly the kind of self-righteous shit I would have pulled when I was a teenager. During a therapy session many years later, when comparing Lisa's relationship to Homer with my own relationship to my father, I suddenly burst into tears. I couldn't believe I was crying over a cartoon, but it made sense. My father loved me but had no idea who I was, and I, too, lacked the compassion and maturity to understand who *he* was.

WHAT DID *I* want out of life? I sure as hell didn't want to work in a factory. That was my parents' worst nightmare. They hadn't crossed the deadly Tijuana border for their kids to work like donkeys in this country. I know they would have been happy if we simply had white-collar jobs, it didn't matter what kind, but I always knew I wanted so much more than that—ridiculous, impossible things.

I certainly didn't want to get married or have kids. Judging from what I saw in my family, children seemed to suck all the joy out of life. Most of the married women I knew seemed to be unhappy in their marriages, so I fashioned together my dream life from various books and movies. If other women in the world were financially independent, traveled alone, and went to college, why couldn't I?

I GOT MYSELF through college and graduate school without any financial help from my parents. I refused to ask them and burden them further. I pulled through alone—even if it meant I went without a proper coat one year—and I was proud of that. After I got my MFA, I was stuck in corporate America for two grueling years until I was able to cobble together a living by tutoring at a local university and freelance writing for outlets like *Cosmopolitan for Latinas*, NBC News, and *The Guardian*. I was hustling and barely surviving. Though I was successful in many ways, I felt financially disempowered. And in some ways, the financial disempowerment made the success embarrassing. I didn't care what my parents had managed to accomplish on similar means, I was supposed to be doing better than that. I had been poor for most of my life, and I was tired. Accolades were nice, but I wanted my success to translate into cold hard cash in my little brown hands. I wanted the luxury of buying a pair of shoes without falling into a spiral of worry and guilt.

I got married the summer I turned thirty. During that time, my writing had garnered the attention of a public relations firm, and they offered me a full-time, salaried position as a senior strategist. Much of my writing would be focused on reproductive rights, which I had been passionate about since I was a teen, and it was more money than I had ever seen in my life. It was not my dream job, not by any means—I imagined I'd be a professor or famous writer by thirty (ha!)—but I was excited to write about issues I cared about, and I was eager to be compensated for my knowledge and talent. Though I could still live in Chicago, the job would require me to travel frequently to New York. I had always been scrappy, and I'd traveled to many places on my own. I felt like I could do anything.

AFTER MY FIRST DAY, I went back to my work-provided apartment on the Upper West Side shaky and scared. That's all I remember. That and a futon in the living room that smelled overwhelmingly of man parts. Every night afterward, I woke up drenched in sweat. Sometimes I would meet friends after work and cry over dinner. Fortunately, I was in Manhattan and no one cared that a grown woman was weeping into her Kung Pao chicken. The man walking down the street with a cat perched on his head and the drunk woman stumbling about in fishnet panties were much more interesting.

When I returned to New York the second time, I began to lose my mind. It was as if some wires were crossed in my brain. I was suddenly so tense that I forgot how to breathe at a normal pace. "I don't know how to breathe anymore," I told my husband in a panic.

THE MOST APPALLING component of the company's structure was a time-tracking system called Time Task. Essentially, we were all required to account for every minute of the day. If I switched tasks—say, from a press release to discussing another client with a coworker—I was expected to stop the timer that kept track of my work on that project and begin a new one to record the length of the conversation about the other client. Our timers were supposed to run all day so that management could monitor what we were doing. Multitasking became excruciating because every inane task had to be documented. We were required to write a description for everything we did throughout the day, and by the time we left for the day, we had to account for at least eight hours of work done in the office. If your time didn't add up, if there were any gaps, there was going to be trouble.

Not only was using Time Task humiliating, it triggered episodes of severe anxiety. I couldn't sleep. I lost weight. I cried in the bathroom. I secretly took my husband's antianxiety drugs just to get through the day. I had fought so hard to create the kind of life I wanted for myself—a life of art and freedom—and now I was stuck at a job that controlled my every move. It terrified me. And though it paid far beyond my parents' meager factory wages, I was, in some ways, treated like they were—my boss was exacting and condescending, and I was expected to crank out writing as if I were a machine. I had to finish complex writing projects in unreasonable amounts of time. It filled me with distress. Once, my boss scolded me in front of a coworker for taking notes during a meeting. Another time she made me revise a six-hundred-word document eleven times, which amounted to about nine hours of work. She regarded her own mistakes (the ones that she actually copped to) as innocuous. But the mistakes of others were deeply personal failings. Missteps, both hers and my colleagues', were ours to rectify. She remains one of the worst people I've ever met, an impressive title considering how many assholes I've come across throughout the years.

When I described the office culture and working conditions to a friend of mine, she very accurately called my job "a sweatshop of the mind." I never felt so devalued and disrespected in my entire adult life.

As a perfectionist, I was accustomed to meeting, if not exceeding, expectations. But failure was so clearly built into the job as a perverse incentive for improving performance that not only was I failing, but I was failing *often*. I didn't handle it well. Indeed, not since I was a child had I dealt with the disappointment of failure so gracelessly. Once, in kindergarten, I made a Christmas tree that involved gluing Froot Loops together to form a garland. I didn't like how my tree had turned out—I'd used too much glue, and it was too messy for my taste. I asked my teacher for the opportunity to start over, but she refused. Though she insisted that it looked fine, I was so ashamed of my shitty artwork that I couldn't stop crying. My teacher called my dad to pick me up because I was inconsolable.

Knowing that I wasn't what my parents, culture, or environment expected me to be, that I was in some ways a disappointment, I set incredibly high standards for myself from an early age. I'd always studied hard and approached every interest with devout dedication—fixating on every word of my poetry until I'd found the perfect one, for example. People like me were not expected to succeed, and I intended to prove everybody wrong. And of course, trauma makes some of us overachieve.

I WAS ALWAYS happy to be the hardest-working person in the room, but this job was different. Several weeks into my new role, I had trouble functioning at work and at home. I couldn't pry myself off the couch and would often sleep to escape the turmoil in my brain. I kept my family at a distance because I didn't want to alarm them, and I avoided friends because the mere thought of talking to people exhausted me. I was only a handful of months into my marriage, and it was already beginning to unfurl. It was one of the loneliest times of my life.

My hypercritical boss and the time-tracking system stirred up my issues with authority and control. I resented the situation because it was infantilizing. My environment, once again, wanted me to conform. It wanted me to shut the fuck up.

Fifteen years after my first suicidal episode and here I was, wanting to die again. I thought my writing would give me the freedom to do whatever I wanted, to live the life I had always imagined for myself when I was a girl. But it felt like it was just another trap.

QUITTING NEVER SEEMED like an option to me, though I knew that this work environment would continue to destroy me. I tried at first to negotiate a better work situation for myself by suggesting I work as their consultant instead, but the scraps they offered to pay me could not have sustained a life in Chicago. One evening, I unleashed all my anger and frustration in an epic phone call with my boss. I paced my apartment, fuming, and outlined all the ways that their family business was fucked up, and then I quit. It was such a catharsis, the kind of thing you fantasize about but doubt you'll ever do. Still, quitting felt like failing. I saw myself as a resilient woman, and yet I couldn't survive this. *Who the hell do you think you are?* I asked myself again and again. After all my parents had survived to raise us, my inability to handle an office job, no matter how oppressive, felt shameful.

I was afraid to tell my mom I had quit the highest-paying job I'd ever had, but once I did, she was relieved rather than disappointed. She had seen the toll it had taken on my mental health. "Tu si eres chingona," my mother said to me when I shared the news. It's only now that I can see the irony of her compliment: "chingona," a badass bitch—literally, a woman who fucks. I had defied her attempts to shelter me, and she had somehow learned to admire that. I understood then that I would never be a failure to my mother. We'd spent so many years bickering and misunderstanding each other that I hadn't realized that in the end, I had made her exceedingly proud.

A FEW WEEKS after I left my job, an international organization I'd previously worked with offered me a consulting project in Trinidad. I was sent there to report on cervical cancer prevention and interview low-income women benefiting from a lifesaving procedure. I was being paid to travel and write about a feminist issue I cared about; it was one of the most exciting opportunities of my life.

As I stood in the passport line waiting to enter the country, I remembered that only a few weeks before, I was sobbing on my couch, wanting to die. And now here I was in a foreign land, not only functioning but exhilarated by my circumstances, by the life I was able to painstakingly build and rebuild. I was mobile and independent, privileged to make choices my mother could never even fathom. When she crossed that deadly border thirty-eight years before, she was giving me permission to one day cross my own.

I LIKE TO ENJOY

After her father was murdered, my grandmother washed his bloody clothes in the river. When I first heard this story on a visit to Mexico in my late twenties, I imagined my young grandmother sobbing as she scrubbed the clothes against the river rocks, the blood dyeing the water red and pink. It wasn't until years later that I wondered why they didn't just throw them away.

YEARS AGO, I called my grandmother from my parents' house to wish her a happy birthday. She's about ninety now and has been in poor health for as long as I can remember. She has endured hardships that are inconceivable to me. As a young woman, she was so poor that she worked as a maid in a teacher's home, and when she married my grandfather at the age of eighteen, they celebrated with cookies and hot chocolate on the morning of their wedding, as it was all they could afford. And though it's beautiful in a way, I don't sentimentalize it.

My grandmother had seven children, not including the few who died. There were times when she couldn't afford salt or chicken feed. One afternoon, while sitting at the kitchen table in their home in Mexico, my aunt told me a story to illustrate the extent of our family's poverty: After a big party, my grandmother's sister-in-law gave her platters of leftovers to feed her children. When my grandmother was about to serve the food the following day, she discovered it was filled with toothpicks, napkins, and other debris. It turns out that this woman had given my grandmother the scraps that people had left on their plates. I can't imagine enduring that kind of humiliation, to be served food that was usually fed to pigs or thrown away. I grew up in an apartment full of roaches, and at times there was no hot water, but this was something else entirely.

As I held the phone to my ear, I mouthed to my parents, "Does she know about the divorce?" They nodded. Typically, my grandmother is shielded from this sort of bad news because she tends to literally worry herself sick. I'm notoriously terrible at pretending—the truth is always written in my voice and on my face—so I was relieved that I didn't have to dance around her questions.

My grandmother asked me about the state of my life, wanted to know why my ex and I couldn't work it out. I gave a vague response, because it was impossible to tell this truth succinctly, to explain why after eight and a half years together and only a year and a half of marriage, I knew our relationship couldn't be salvaged. Like any elderly Mexican lady, she expressed concern for my age. To be divorced and childless at the age of thirty-two is unheard of in my family. I assured her that I was looking for a partner and that I wasn't too old to bear children, and that despite my obstacles and empty womb, I was happy with my life. My grandmother didn't seem convinced, however, and expressed concern about my vagabond ways. That's the reputation I have in my family—a restless woman who does as she pleases. I've never lived by anyone's rules and can't sit still, which has always exasperated my parents and perplexed everyone else. I've moved and traveled so many times that I stopped keeping track. I think my grandmother pictures me perpetually holding a suitcase. Her nickname for me is "golondrina," which means "swallow." I have a swallow tattooed on my forearm in homage to her. In the song "Las Golondrinas," by Pedro Infante, a tired bird travels in search of a home. The speaker in the song is also lost, but he's unable to fly, and he offers la golondrina a space to build her nest inside his own heart.

I wasn't offended by my grandmother's inquiries about my romantic life, because I knew they came from a place of love. She has always been one of my most loyal defenders. When I was visiting her one summer as a teenager, I overheard her talking about me when she thought I was still asleep. She told whoever she was speaking to that I was wise and special but misunderstood. I was touched by this because at that age, I felt that no one saw me in a way that was compassionate or even remotely accurate.

My grandmother's name is Clara, which means "clear," and that's what she has always been to me; her love is unconditional and never complicated.

As I attempted to explain myself to her, I realized how impossible it was to do so. My life has always been defined by letters, words, and books. Since the age of twelve, all I ever wanted was to be a writer. Here I was, building my career, in many ways living my childhood dreams, but she seemed to think that my life was falling apart. And who could blame her? My grandmother never had a formal education, never learned to read or write, and has spent her entire life in a town where everyone knows her name. When I think about the gap between us, sometimes I'm astonished.

Family is what matters most to my grandmother, and I understand. I desired my own family, too, that sense of belonging. It's part of why I left my marriage. But until I built a family, I planned to keep leading an indulgent life. I'm not sure I could ever explain this to my grandmother, though, that I essentially do whatever the fuck I want to do, that I've spent an ungodly amount of time and money pursuing my pleasures. This is a woman who didn't have enough food to feed her family, and I had just taken a trip to Europe simply because I wanted to.

WHEN PEOPLE ASKED me why Portugal, I didn't have a good answer. I booked the trip one night on an impulse. It sounded safe enough for a woman traveling alone, and I was on the verge of receiving the first part of my novel advance. I joked that I was on some *Eat, Pray, Love* shit, except I wasn't a rich white lady. I had been wanting to take a trip for months but kept talking myself out of it, had a million reasons not to—student loans, divorce, bills, moving, and so on. But part of me felt that I deserved the trip after both of my books had been accepted for publication. I had been waiting twenty years for this to happen and hadn't had the chance to celebrate because I received the news as I was about to leave my husband.

Some say that after a divorce, people often spend large sums of money on something frivolous in an attempt to reclaim their life, and I suppose that's what I was doing. Two weeks after I booked the flight, I was in Lisbon without any concrete plans.

THE CITY WAS in beautiful decay. Old ornate buildings had long been abandoned and were sprouting weeds from the rooftops, from nearly every crack and crevice. The ubiquitous graffiti added a sort of texture and bright grittiness I'm often drawn to. The blight says we're all transients here. I've always loved the way nature can reclaim spaces; the resilience and tenacity make me hopeful. I believe it should humble us, remind us how temporary and insignificant we are, not only on this planet, but in the entire universe. *What the fuck do we matter in the grand scheme of things?* I often wonder. While this idea used to paralyze me, I now find it comforting. I take refuge in the idea of eternity.

Some people I encountered were perplexed by the sight of a woman traveling alone. There were times I also wondered what the hell I was doing with my life and felt a pang of guilt as I sipped a glass of Vinho Verde on a terrace. I had no one to answer to, which was both liberating and daunting. Who gave me permission to be this person?

In the style of insufferable romantic comedies about women

"finding" themselves in foreign lands, I was eager to get laid and have a sexy adventure, but that was proving difficult. It seemed there were no viable suitors. I considered having sex with my first Airbnb host until he told me he was "writing a book about his life," a guaranteed way to vanquish my desires. He also told me his favorite writer was Paulo Coelho, and by then I was closed for business. "Fechada," I told a friend back home. There was a fellow who accompanied me on a day trip to Sintra, a fairy-tale village outside Lisbon, but he was neither attractive nor interesting, so I politely abandoned him after a while.

One afternoon, I walked to an old fortress at the top of the city. It was a stunning view of the bridges, bright buildings, and terracotta roofs. I tried to enjoy the weather and the gorgeous sites and did my best to suppress my loneliness when I saw couples, families, and groups of friends. I walked up and down the narrow staircases and snapped pictures of the castle. As I worked my way back down the hill, I saw a gaggle of loud adolescents. I considered turning around and walking in the opposite direction. Groups of children sometimes overwhelm me, and I'm embarrassed to admit that I worried they'd say something mean-spirited. Then it struck me how absurd this was: I was literally *afraid of children*. I decided against finding a new route and kept walking. As I passed the group, one of them yelled, "Bella," and another said, "Beautiful," wistfully, as if she were in disbelief. For a moment I wondered who they were talking about and then realized they were referring to me.

I became filled with shame. I didn't know how to respond to these sweet children, so I just smiled and continued. I was stunned.

It was then that I understood that I had spent so much of my life bracing myself for pain, discomfort, and humiliation.

THAT NIGHT I got dressed up and went to a traditional fado club in a charming and labyrinthine part of the city. I was already in love with the beautifully mournful music. I sat by myself near the stage and sipped on my port, trying not to feel self-conscious. Though I wasn't embarrassed about being alone, I knew that many people feel pity for unaccompanied women. I shouldn't care, but I prefer not to be studied, and I get tired of the questions. *Why are you by yourself? Where is your husband? Aren't you afraid to travel alone?* Sometimes it's as if the world thinks you're irrelevant—silly, even—when you're a solitary woman.

The music was striking and it stirred up a jumble of emotions. Part of me felt as if my soul were being purged. It was similar to the feeling I had when I watched flamenco in Spain—a deep and satisfying ache. I wondered if this beauty, like duende, was also born from its proximity to death. Or was it the acknowledgment of loss? Are they the same thing? It was one of the most transformative sounds I'd ever heard, and there were moments I thought my insides would burst. In that anguished state of satisfaction, I noticed a dull couple look at me and then at each other. I felt them judge me, feel sorry for me. But it was I who pitied them, because it was clear that they had reached the stage in their relationship where they were profoundly bored of each other, where they desperately searched for something to talk about because they'd exhausted every topic. That's why I was so interesting to them. I recognized it because I've lived it.

"Fado" comes from the Latin word for "fate" or "destiny." They say "saudade" is untranslatable, but it's a word that feels like an old, familiar cloak to me, because I've spent so much of my life ravenous for both past and future. Saudade is described a number of ways: longing for one's homeland, longing for the past, longing for something that doesn't exist or never existed, longing for a beloved who is gone. A hope for something you can't control. An absence that becomes a presence. An existential wound. A delicious longing. A joyful sorrow. A profound nostalgia. According to the Portuguese writer Francisco Manuel de Melo, saudade is "a pleasure you suffer, an ailment that you enjoy." Sometimes you carry the sadness because you don't want to let go of the person you desire, even if you know they're never coming back, even though carrying them inside you makes you throb with sorrow. Like duende, it's a wound that never heals. For me it feels like being in love with a ghost. It's relishing hurt. Worshipping a void. I've done this my whole life.

I SPENT MOST of my time in Portugal in various cities getting lost, writing in my journal, stuffing my face with pastries, and drinking wine. I wandered in a constant state of awe. By the time I reached Porto, the last city on my itinerary, I had given up hope on a European romance. I had just had a date with a man who said he'd read only two books in his entire life, and I was disillusioned.

(At first I wondered if it was the language barrier, but I soon realized he was just stupid. Once he told me he wrote poetry, I became hostile and left.)

I got to my hotel and changed quickly. I was sweaty and running out of clothes. My body was damp, my underwear fragrant, but I didn't want to waste time taking a shower because I had only twenty-four hours to explore Porto.

I stood at the corner of the street debating where to eat when I saw a handsome man with a lustrous beard serving drinks at a café. He had an anachronistic air about him—tall and thin, wearing a black vest and porkpie hat. I decided to have lunch there and felt him looking at me as I ate my meal, and decided to ask him if he had plans that evening. At that point, I was feeling bold and had nothing left to lose.

His name was Filipe, and as he gave me a tour of Porto later that evening, he lamented that I hadn't visited sooner. It was one of the most romantic places I had ever seen: the aesthetic was a sort of withered nostalgia, as if the city itself were longing for a time that no longer existed. Neither of us could stop smiling. He took me to see the beautiful blue-tiled walls at the train station, pointed out stunning architecture, and took pictures of me smiling on the Dom Luís I Bridge. At one point, we stopped at a public square where a group of people were dancing tango. As Filipe went to get his car to drive us to the beach, I stood there gaping at all the cheerful couples and reflected on my good fortune. The moment seemed too pleasurable, too cinematic to be real.

We sat at a bar near the ocean and drank beer in the late

afternoon sun. It was Sunday and many families were out together enjoying the day. Nervous, I guzzled my giant glass of beer within minutes and ordered another. I was so self-conscious that I didn't even want to eat the olives set in front of us, afraid of how I'd look chewing them. We tried our best to understand each other in Spanish, which he wasn't quite fluent in, because my Portuguese was hopeless.

The sun was beginning to set and the air was almost cool as we walked back to the car. A gust of wind blew Filipe's hat off his head, and I thought it was cute the way we scrambled after it. When he retrieved it and caught up to me, we both turned to each other and kissed with total disregard for the people around us. It was frantic, almost frenzied. I had wanted this story so much that I invented all sorts of feelings.

We were stuck in traffic as we drove to his apartment. What would normally be a fifteen-minute trip took over an hour. We held hands and made out when the car was stopped. Filipe said all the clichéd things I needed to hear: He felt connected to me. He liked my smile. I was special. Maybe we had met in another life, I suggested. I couldn't believe such drivel was coming out of my mouth.

I looked at the darkening sky and told myself to remember this moment. Dusk has always been my favorite time of day—the softness of the light, the sound of crickets and cicadas. There's a calm in the quiet humming, a suspense that excites me. It's the hour when most people begin to wind down and partake in their pleasures. One of the most enjoyable experiences is taking a walk at twilight when the smells of dinner are wafting through the streets.

When we approached Filipe's neighborhood, we stopped by a grocery store to pick up some dinner. It was all very European—cheese, olives, pâté, bread, and gelato. We were giddy—couldn't stop touching each other—and I could only imagine how obnoxious we must have seemed to the other customers waiting in line.

Filipe and I had sex after we ate and we continued through the night and well into the morning. Although in retrospect the sex was mediocre (lots of careless thrusting), I made myself believe that it was amazing. My hot European fantasy had come to fruition. Oh, the lies we tell ourselves.

The next morning we had espresso and toast at a nearby café. We held hands and kissed in the streets. We had sex a few more times in his apartment before he drove me to the bus station. Filipe told me he wished I could stay, what a shame it was that we had met at the very end of my trip. He asked me to return so he could take me to his family's vineyard and said he would give me a tour of the wine country. He told me he'd visit me in Chicago in the fall, during his slow season. A man took our picture before I boarded the bus. The sun was bright and we looked like a happy couple.

I returned to Chicago with romantic notions of a transatlantic love affair. I felt vibrant and sexy, which was the opposite of what I'd felt at the end of my marriage.

Filipe and I continued to chat online, sometimes with video. We said we missed each other and concocted plans to meet again. One night, after I'd been back home for two weeks, he told me that he had spent the weekend fucking his girlfriend. For a second, I very stupidly wondered if I had perhaps misunderstood because of the language barrier. Fucking his girlfriend? That couldn't be. But when I asked him to clarify, he said it again.

Though I didn't consider Filipe my boyfriend, I never saw this coming. I had studied his apartment and there was no trace of woman—no hair ties, stray makeup, or extra toothbrush.

I stared at my laptop in disbelief. I kept asking him to explain why he would lie to me and his girlfriend. What kind of person was he?

Filipe maintained that he had done nothing wrong and meant everything he'd said. He still cared about me and wanted to see me again. Why? I persisted. I grew more and more exasperated trying to reason with him.

"I like to enjoy," he finally said to me.

And what do you say to that?

I SOBBED THAT night and part of the next morning. It wasn't that I was in love with this man I barely knew. It was that he had disappointed me, like every other man had. Toward the afternoon, however, I started to find the humor in it, had told several of my friends about "I like to enjoy." It quickly became one of our most popular catchphrases. It was so absurd I couldn't even be angry anymore. I'd been thinking I was living a sappy romantic comedy and this man was lying to me and his girlfriend.

Just as I was beginning to let go of the whole ordeal, I received a Facebook message from Filipe's girlfriend. I was now entangled in some international drama. She included a screenshot of messages between Filipe and a friend of his. They were in Portuguese, but I was able to translate them with the help of the internet. In the exchange Filipe bragged about having sex with me. He said I was a "crazy American nymphomaniac who wanted to have sex all night and day." His girlfriend wanted to know if this was true, if Filipe and I had had sex. Of course it was true, I told her. Was more evidence really needed?

Her response surprised me. "Thank you," she wrote, and I never heard from her again.

I called my friend Sara that afternoon and told her the story. I felt so used and objectified, I bemoaned.

"No," she assured me. "Don't. You just have an internationally renowned pussy."

WHEN I FIRST moved out of my parents' house as a senior in college, one of my uncles told his daughter to stay away from me. He said I was a bad influence and that he didn't want me to be part of her life. My crime? I had taken my cousin to Chipotle one evening to encourage her to go to college. The irony was stupefying to me. According to my uncle, I was a bad woman because I lived alone and had traveled to Mexico with my boyfriend the summer before. This was coming from a man who had led a double life. For years my uncle had carried on an affair with a woman and had a child with her.

That is how threatening a solitary woman is to the flimsy idea of masculinity.

In the essay "The Sons of Malinche," Octavio Paz, arguably a misogynist in his own right, unpacks this deep-seated notion of women in the Mexican psyche. "When passive, she becomes a goddess, a beloved one, a being who embodies the ancient, stable elements of the universe: the earth, motherhood, virginity. When active, she is always function and means, a receptacle and a channel. Womanhood, unlike manhood, is never an end in itself." We are not allowed to be human beings, agents of our own existence, because we've been forced to be symbols of our entire culture. But what if we reject this responsibility? What if we say fuck this shit and light everything on fire?

"The Mexican considers woman to be a dark, secret, and passive being," Paz continues. "He does not attribute evil instincts to her; he even pretends she does not have any." Or, to put it more exactly, her instincts are not her own but those of the species, because she is an incarnation of the life force, which is essentially impersonal. Thus it is impossible for her to have a private life, for if she were to be herself—if she were to be the mistress of her own wishes, passions, or whims—she would be unfaithful to herself.

I BEGAN MOVING into my new apartment on the south side of Chicago about a month after I told my husband that I wanted a divorce. When I walked through the door, I said to myself, out loud, "I will be happy here." It was more a promise than a wish. It was the first time in my life I was living completely on my own. I've always had to share a space in some form or other, and though my divorce was devastating, the idea of being untethered to anyone was almost intoxicating to me.

Living alone turned out to be pleasurable in a multitude of ways, but I soon discovered that I was bad at feeding myself. There were times I ate nothing but canned trout and crackers for dinner. Once I ate chips and a bowl of dip and then fell asleep crying on my couch. I was unmotivated to care for myself in a real adult way. Eating alone felt like a chore, and there was no one to judge the way I lived. (It's worth noting that when I began writing this essay, I still didn't own a saltshaker or an iron.) Despite this, I insisted it was my renaissance.

I loved staying up late reading and writing. I paced around my apartment as I wrote poems. I blared whatever music I pleased. I read poetry aloud. I watched obscure movies in the middle of the night.

During the first few months, I dated with abandon. I wanted so much to be wanted. Most of the encounters were empty—I hadn't figured out that I needed an emotional connection to have a truly satisfying sexual experience—but I still enjoyed the thrill of touching a stranger's body, of letting someone inside me.

One afternoon my cat unearthed a used condom from under my bed. As I stared at it in the middle of the living room, I realized I wasn't sure who it had belonged to. I was slut-shamed by my cat.

In *A Room of One's Own*, Virginia Woolf writes: "All the conditions of her life, all her own instincts, were hostile to the state of mind which is needed to set free whatever is in the brain." What did freedom mean to me? The space and time to create art. To be alone. To read. To wonder. To experiment. Though Woolf couldn't have conceived of a person like me, her words illuminated so much of my reality—the innate love for words that had always dictated my life. When I was a kid, my mother worried that I read too much, spent too much time alone. I'd be engrossed in a book for hours, getting lost in fictional worlds, ignoring my responsibilities and surroundings. There was something about these places in my imagination—a sense of unlimited possibility that I couldn't find anywhere else.

My life has been defined by poetry but was never conducive to creating it. There was nothing in my environment that encouraged this vocation. As a teenager, I constantly fought for my solitude, and as a daughter of working-class immigrants, this art form seemed like an indulgence to everyone, including myself. Sometimes I still wonder why, of all things, I loved words so much. Who could have passed this down to me?

Women need money to thrive intellectually, Woolf insists. This will always be true. Some of the most miserable times in my life were spent at the mind-numbing office jobs I took out of desperation. Anything that kept me from reading and writing felt like a punishment, because I was always aware that I was squandering my talents.

I often consider all the working-class women who have inherent gifts they must suppress in order to survive and feed their families. My mother, for example, is an intellectually curious woman, but she worked the night shift at a factory and never had a moment to herself, let alone time to read a book. I wonder who she could have become in a different context.

Though I was not rich by any means at this point in my life, I had won a generous poetry fellowship, which helped keep me afloat. I had also saved a significant amount of my income while working that white-collar PR job that nearly destroyed my spirit, and like I mentioned, I had just received part of my novel advance. I had sacrificed so much in order to live this way, worked my ass off, but I was undoubtedly privileged. Writing this very essay would have been impossible without the luxury of privacy and silence.

MY RELATIONSHIP WITH my maternal grandmother, Luisa, is fraught. She's hated me since I was a child and never tried to hide it. I still don't know precisely why—I suspect it was envy—but needless to say, I don't love her. Regardless, I do try to empathize with her, because I know that she's suffered. As with most Mexican women of her time, marriage was typically the only option. Going to school or having a career was simply not on the table. And women were expected to endure all suffering in silence.

Recently, my mom told me that as a child, my grandmother enjoyed learning and wanted to go to school but that my great-grandmother pulled her out and forced her, literally, to make tortillas for the family instead. My grandmother was excited to learn how to write the word "Faro," the old brand of unfiltered cigarettes, when she was forced to quit her education. She still gets angry when she tells this story, my mother says. Hearing this was the first time I'd ever feel a true connection to my grandmother.

Eventually, my grandmother did teach herself basic reading and writing. My grandfather sent her letters while laboring as a migrant worker in the Bracero Program in the United States. My grandmother got tired of asking people to read them to her, so she took it upon herself to figure it out.

Woolf is right about many of the conditions that hinder women writers; however, I disagree with her view on rage in our writing. According to Woolf, a woman's anger compromises the integrity of her art. But all my favorite writers are furious in some form or other. Why shouldn't they be? And who would I even be without my indignation? I nurse my rage. I name it. I hold it close to me. I brush its hair and sing it lullabies.

When I visited Paris at the age of twenty-two, I remember reading a postcard that said something like "The fire that burns me is the fire that feeds me." I don't remember who or where the quote comes from, but that notion has been nestled in my brain for fifteen years now.

I SAW FRANCISCO GOYA for the second time at the Blanton Museum of Art at the University of Texas at Austin one summer. I had loved his work since I'd lived in Madrid, but as I stood before *Still Life with Golden Bream*, I was newly mesmerized. I stared at it with wide eyes and muttered to myself, as I often do when overwhelmed by beauty. "Holy fucking shit," I said to no one. Though the fish were lifeless, they were wildly iridescent. Their eyes were at once dead and perceptive. These moments are spiritual for me. I don't believe in God per se, but I do believe in transcendence. This is when I feel most alive, most aware of the human capacity for brilliance.

I reflected on how lucky I was to spend an afternoon gawking at art in another city.

One of the exhibits that season was titled *Book from the Sky*, by Chinese artist Xu Bing. The installation consisted of printed text in the form of scrolls, books, and wall panels. The words appeared to be real, but they were completely imagined.

The made-up language fascinated me; I was enamored with the words even though they meant nothing. It was different than appreciating a foreign tongue, because this text held no meaning for even its creator, the artist. As I studied the pieces, I wondered about my ancestors, all the women who came before me, and I considered what it would be like to experience the world without the gift of the written language, something that has been so instrumental to my survival. So much of my power has depended on my manipulation of words. Who would I be without them?

Bing once wrote about his installation: "Any doctoring of the written word results in transformation at the core of a person's thinking. . . . My approach is filled with reverence, yet mixed with mockery; as I tease [the written word], I also hold it above the altar."

THERE'S A TV SERIES that I love about the life of Sor Juana Inés de la Cruz, a writer, nun, and feminist of colonial Mexico. It's full of scandal, dramatic in the style of telenovelas. Though I had studied her in college, I wasn't fully aware of her fierceness until I began watching the show and fell down a rabbit hole of research. I've always been intrigued by solitary women like her. In high school, I wore white dresses in homage to Emily Dickinson. I was captivated by Sor Juana's love of learning, the way she was willing to compromise everything in order to read, write, and wonder.

Sor Juana's crime was that she was a woman who questioned, who refused to shut up and obey, and the colonial culture she lived in ultimately forced her to make an excruciating choice: renounce her studies or be expelled from the church. It still wrecks me that she had to apologize for who she was. As I watched her study her empty bookshelves, I considered what life would be without my books. I don't mean to sound precious or romantic—I mean this literally—but I don't think I would survive it.

"Yo, la peor de todas," she lamented toward the end of her life. Whether she truly believed it or was simply giving the church the spectacle they wanted, we will never know. In the essay "The Conquest and Colonialism," Octavio Paz writes of Sor Juana, "The lonely figure of Sor Juana became more and more isolated in the world of affirmations and negotiations, a world that denied the value of doubt and inquiry." That's the fate of so many women—being perpetually alone in their quest to think outside binaries, to revel in nuance and ambiguity. Paz continues, "We can sense the melancholy of a spirit who never succeeded in forgiving herself for her boldness and her condition as a woman." Sor Juana's genius is now undisputed, but she suffered for it. I'd like to believe that she didn't see her life as a mistake. After her death, it was discovered that she had never stopped writing, and although this work was not public in her lifetime, it was her rebellion.

MY PARENTS LIKE to joke about what the state of my life would be if they had never crossed the border. I also wonder. Would I still be me? Would I have adapted to my environment? Maybe I wouldn't exist at all.

My mom knows how miserable I'd be without access to an education or the freedom to move through the world on my own. If I were a version of who I am now, stuck in my parents' hometown, I'd be beyond desperate.

When I complained about my lack of dating prospects, my mother would say, "Imagine if you had grown up in el rancho." The image of me as a housewife with lots of children in rural Mexico is both ridiculous and amusing to her. She jokes about it a lot.

"Ya hubiera matado dos or tres cabrones," my father said once, and we laughed and laughed.

AS I GREW up in traditional Mexican culture, sex was portrayed as something that was done to you. For a woman, it was an act to be endured. The only power we had was holding it over someone in order to manipulate them. There was never any talk of female pleasure, never any acknowledgment that we were active agents in the process. At school, sex ed was limited to lessons on anatomy and shaming tactics. Girls were advised to keep their legs closed. It's no wonder that it has taken me my whole adult life to undo this damage, to convince myself that I deserve joy in all its incarnations. This isn't simply a result of my Catholic upbringing, though that played a significant role; much of it stems from my status as a woman of color in this country, what I was raised to expect from the world. What did I have a right to? Who was I to demand so much? We continue to be one of the most underpaid demographics in the United States, making fifty-five cents to every white man's dollar. As I was coming of age, most depictions of Latinas in the media were so dehumanizing; they were either meek and poor or hypersexualized to a cartoonish degree. (This is beginning to change, but much too slowly.) There was no complexity, no sense of agency. In many contexts, particularly in romantic relationships, I learned to accept dregs.

I spent the year after my divorce convincing myself not only that I was entitled to nice things, but that the nice things I *did* have would not be taken away. As a child, I learned that I had to protect my belongings. I lived in a place where people would steal the Jordans off your feet, so I'm hypervigilant about what I own. People who leave their doors unlocked perplex me to no end. This has trickled into other realms of my life.

Though highly educated and accomplished, sometimes I feel a lingering dread that everything will be snatched away one day and I will be left destitute. I still have a recurring nightmare in which I'm suddenly informed that I never graduated from college because I'm missing several credits. As a result, I have to re-enroll and take the necessary steps to get my degree. In some of these dreams, I have to return to high school. Somehow, I forget about my classes and fail the semester. I always wake up startled and relieved.

I believe this points to an anxiety beyond impostor syndrome. It's not that I believe myself to be fake or unworthy, it's that I question whether a person like me will be allowed to live the way I choose. I have always known that there was something special about me, a part I wanted to share with the world, but my fear was that the world wouldn't see it or wouldn't care.

The year I lived in Spain, I spent several days alone in Paris. I walked along the Seine with no sense of direction one beautiful afternoon. It was spring and though I'd never had allergies before, something in the air made my eyes water uncontrollably during my entire stay. I kept wiping them with the back of my hand, hoping no one thought I was weeping in the streets.

As I studied the river and Gothic architecture, it suddenly struck me that I had gotten myself to Paris. I was alone in a different country, something I had always dreamt about as a child. It was then that the real crying began. I was so overwhelmed by the realization that I wept tears of joy for the first time in my life.

AFTER I LEFT MY HUSBAND, I went on so many terrible dates. Most men didn't make it past the first date because I was so sure of what I didn't want. Once I left a date before we even got to the restaurant because he told me that he lived with his mom and that his ex-girlfriend was trying to get back together with him. I told him to drive me home immediately. A year into online dating, I had written it off completely. I didn't believe I would find the love of my life by swiping right. A few weeks later, I downloaded Tinder again, as I was lonely and meeting suitors in your thirties is complicated.

As a writer, I've always been concerned with living good stories. I didn't like the thought of someone asking me how I met my spouse and admitting that our matchmaker was the internet. That, to me, was not a sexy story. All year I fantasized about meet-cutes—falling for a beautiful stranger at a bookstore or library, on a train or plane. We'd lock eyes as we browsed the cultural criticism section. One of us would crack a joke and then we'd spend the afternoon discussing race and gender over many cups of coffee. Some shit like that.

I agreed to drinks with an allegedly handsome man on Tinder one evening at a hipster cocktail bar with vinyl booths and dim lighting. By then I thought I had learned to lower my expectations but not my standards. I had been deceived by flattering and outdated photographs many times before. I was already equipped with an excuse to leave early if I wasn't feeling it. My go-to: I had to get to bed early because I had a writing deadline. Of course there was no deadline—anyone could see right through it—but I had been on so many dates that I no longer cared. I was efficient and didn't want to waste my time or anyone else's.

As it happened, I didn't need my deadline excuse. My date was tall and handsome, much more attractive in person than in his pictures. He made me laugh and I liked the way he looked at me, as if I were the only person in the room.

"I bet a lot of men are afraid of your strong personality," he said.

"Yes," I agreed. "They really are."

He smiled. "Well, I like it."

Though I was not enamored, we ended the night with tacos, and tacos for me are always a good omen, a sign of promise. We kissed briefly and planned to meet again.

We went out a few more times and I soon slipped into a bout of depression and lost interest in him—and everything else, for that matter. I felt like a wisp of a person. I called him one night and explained that I was struggling with my mental health and didn't think I had anything to give at the moment. I didn't expect to cry, but my voice cracked as I said it, and the tears began. His voice was quiet and I could hear his disappointment, but he said he understood and wished me well. I cried on the couch a long time after that.

I think there were myriad reasons for this slump, a perfect storm of shittiness to make me want to curl up and disappear into myself. This was right after the 2016 presidential election, and I had lost hope in humanity. What was the point of anything? I wondered. What kind of world did I have to live in now? How could I be so naive that I hadn't seen this coming? I couldn't make sense of anything and read the news in a state of horror. Every morning I'd wake up hoping it was all a nightmare.

This was also right after Thanksgiving, and I've always had a hard time with the darkness, the cold, and the holidays. Christmas season fills me with gloom. I find the cheerful music and the commercialism insufferable.

It was exactly one year since I had left my husband, and the year before that, 2014, I had gone through another bout of depression so severe that I contemplated suicide. I thought a lot about my failed relationships and realized I had never been loved the way I needed to be. Perhaps something was innately wrong with me. The men in my life were always so disappointing. I had been pining for an old coworker of mine all year—a man who was literally dying from an incurable lung disease and had explicitly told me he didn't want to be with me. It was beyond naive; it was masochistic.

My sadness scared me, so I made changes that, in retrospect, simplified my life in profound ways. I cut out alcohol, because my hangovers were always brutal and left me both hopeless and useless. Though I'd never considered myself an alcoholic, and I had decreased my intake in the past few years, I knew it was a problem and understood that I had replicated this kind of dynamic in other realms of my life. I stayed in relationships that I knew were destructive, unhealthy, and abusive, hoping that something would magically change. It was like gorging on poison and expecting not to die.

I started swimming to boost my energy and calm my frayed nerves. Something about being in water was therapeutic, and I began to feel stronger both physically and mentally. I was determined to claw my way out of this hole with every method at my disposal. I delved deeper into my Buddhist practice and chanted with more conviction. There were times I could hardly recite the mantra because I was sobbing too hard. One evening as I was chanting, I had an epiphany that had eluded me my whole life. I had always ached for someone to notice me, to see that I was extraordinary, but did I truly believe that about myself?

During this time, Marcus, the handsome man from Tinder, would check in on me and ask how I was doing. He texted me a funny baby picture of himself on Christmas, and asked if I was free on New Year's Eve. I brushed him off, replied tersely. Though I wasn't interested in him romantically, I didn't want to discard him like I had all the other men I had dated. He said he wanted to know me, even as a friend, because he thought I was an amazing person. It seemed sincere, so I agreed to meet him for dinner again. A man interested in me as a human being? Well, that was rare.

In the fog of my depression, I had forgotten that he was attractive, but that very obvious fact struck me as I walked toward him. And again, he made me laugh, and again, he lavished me with praise, none of which felt false or calculated. Still, I reiterated I didn't want a romantic relationship—I was still feeling fragile—and though he was disappointed once more, he agreed to be friends.

A few days later, Marcus came over to my apartment to watch a stand-up special he thought I would like. He was right—Paul Mooney's takedown of white people made me laugh so hard my stomach hurt. I clapped my hands and kicked my feet. I nodded vigorously in agreement. The jokes were the salve I needed at that moment in my life, in history.

As Marcus hugged me goodbye, it felt good to be wanted. We kissed for a few seconds, but I became uncomfortable, so I showed him the door. "Time for you to go," I laughed, but I was completely serious.

We began dating after that. After a year of being single, he seemed like the best option for me. Though my depression was definitely a major factor in breaking up with Marcus a few months prior, I also couldn't really imagine myself with him. Something about him didn't seem right, though I couldn't articulate what. A tiny worm of doubt wiggled in my mind. I know this sounds strange, but I didn't like the way he smelled. Instead of following my initial instinct, I convinced myself that this was what I had been looking for.

I had struggled to have an orgasm all year. I'd had a few with the dying man months before, but that came with a price. Every time I saw him I was pulled into a cycle of yearning and rejection. I wanted him, but he wanted only parts of me. I knew he was unwilling to commit to even the possibility of a relationship, because he had said it, but once again, I continued to gorge on the poison as if it were cake.

There were times I thought I might be physically broken. I'd had orgasms with ease before my marriage. In high school, all I needed was to rub myself against a boy while we were making out and bam, my underwear was drenched. Why, then, was it so hard for me as a grown woman in her supposed sexual peak? I'd read the book *Vagina* by Naomi Wolf twice at that point, and had learned all about the science, history, and psychology of my own vagina. I was empowered with knowledge: my vagina was *fucking magic*. Plus, I could always get myself off, so it obviously wasn't a physical problem. Was it that the men I had chosen were terrible at sex?

Though I had a lurking doubt in the back of my mind, I enjoyed the attention Marcus gave my body. His tongue was dexterous, and after sex my muscles became limp. I was having the best sex of my life. I had literally prayed for this for an entire year. I had even placed a wooden figurine of a vulva on my altar and chanted to find love and experience pleasure. One night I had an orgasm so deep that my entire body shook.

It wasn't that I was overcome with love or emotion for Marcus, though. I was still feeling skeptical about him. It was that I had given myself permission to escape the shame and inhibition that I had internalized since I was a girl. The pleasure was simple and primal, as if a knot I had been trying to untie since the beginning of time was suddenly pulled loose. I had been waiting to enjoy my body for so long, and the relief of it was staggering.

I understood that unencumbered pleasure was a possibility for me.

It was the only time in my life that I forgot myself, and I wondered if that's what it meant to be free.

DIFFICULT SUN

M any of my childhood dreams came true in my early thirties. After years of toiling and working a string of shitty jobs, all the pieces of my life began to coalesce. I had always been ambitious, but I was painfully aware of how improbable it was for me to make a living off my writing, much less to be acknowledged or celebrated in any measure on account of it. And then, all at once, it was happening.

In August 2017, I moved to Princeton, New Jersey, for my first real teaching gig. I had won the Princeton Arts Fellowship after an intimidating application process, which included several in-person interviews and a party with the other finalists. Several hundred people had applied and I was one of three chosen. I felt like I'd won the Hunger Games. For the first time in my life, I looked forward to going to work. I'm not gonna lie, it was delicious to be a Brown person teaching in an Ivy League university. Not because I believe in these notions of superiority, but because I had invaded a traditionally white space and I wanted to make a muthafuckin' ruckus.

This was also the year that my two books were published to critical acclaim. I had been working on my poetry collection, *Lessons on Expulsion*, for almost a decade, and my debut novel, *I Am Not Your Perfect Mexican Daughter*, was a culmination of about five years' worth of work.

The novel became an instant *New York Times* bestseller and a finalist for the National Book Award before it even came out. I didn't expect both books to be published around the same time, but that's just how it worked out. There were many moments when I wondered, how the fuck is this my life?

The National Book Awards ceremony was like a fairy tale to me. Friends, people in the know, and colleagues described it as "the Oscars of the literary world," and that turned out to be an accurate description. I had never been to such an elegant event. It took place in Manhattan, and not only was the reception visually stunning, many of my literary heroes were in attendance. There are multiple pictures of me grinning on the red carpet that night. I wore an expensive, ostentatious royal-blue gown with a mermaid silhouette, and though I didn't win, it was, hands down, one of the best nights of my life. My books were out in the world and being recognized as something worthwhile; it was surreal.

During this time, I was traveling all over the country to promote the books at readings, literary festivals, and school visits. I'd often wake up not knowing what city I was in. I was exhausted but so satisfied and excited about my life. I was doing what I had always wanted to do.

Everything was coming together for me, including my romantic life. After my failed marriage and many short-lived, dead-end relationships, I had a loving partner who was supportive of my career. This dynamic was foreign to me because my previous partners and suitors had been either resentful or frightened of my ambition and success. My relationship with Marcus was so different than anything that I had ever experienced. He was not my dream man—he didn't have much to offer besides his looks—but he made me feel seen and desired. He enjoyed my assertive personality, liked the challenge that I posed. He thought I was funny, brilliant, and beautiful, and said as much often. We loved each other and though we weren't engaged, we spoke vaguely of getting married and having kids.

I thought I had become the person I was meant to be.

WITH MY NEW FELLOWSHIP came a new psychiatrist, Dr. Petrov, and with her, a new diagnosis. After I'd spent about six months at Princeton, Dr. Petrov diagnosed me as bipolar II. For years, I believed I had the boring kind of depression, but after asking me an endless list of questions, Dr. Petrov determined that I had the fun kind instead. She believed there was no way I could have been so productive with depression. Bipolar disorder was the only explanation. I was aghast. How could this be? Why had no one ever suggested this to me before? I had seen so many doctors since the age of fifteen—the first time I was hospitalized—and it was never presented as even a possibility. The more I thought about it, however, the more sense it made. Though I had never had a full-on manic episode—spending sprees, sex binges, and believing I was Jesus Christ or some shit like that—I've often felt frantic, with too many ideas racing in my head. Expansive. Limitless. It happens a lot when I write. I get so frenzied that I can't sit down. I get short of breath. I'm easily distracted. I pace back and forth and talk to myself. Sometimes I take a nap to quiet my mind.

I've always had extreme mood swings, frustrating my family to no end. As a kid, I was impossible to predict—one minute I was fine and the next I was, well, not. I was aware that I was a pain in the ass, but I couldn't help it. No matter what I did, how I tried to reason with myself, my emotions would overtake me.

I was an expert whiner and undefeated in the sport of crying. I remember visiting relatives in Los Angeles with my mother and two brothers. We went to SeaWorld and watched the whale show from seats toward the back of the arena. I wanted to sit in the front to experience Shamu, that poor captive creature, and when we couldn't, I was so disappointed that I bawled for hours. Instead of being grateful for being there at all—we were poor and this vacation was a huge sacrifice for my parents—I was distraught over something seemingly minute. That my parents couldn't stand me sometimes is understandable.

After all these years, it turned out that what everyone, including me, thought was moodiness was bipolar disorder. As a result of the new diagnosis, Dr. Petrov decided to take me off Prozac, the only medication that had ever worked for me. Instead, I was to take Abilify, an antipsychotic that's used to treat both bipolar disorder and schizophrenia. I was functioning well at that point in my life and had gone to the psychiatrist only for a checkup. Though

I was somewhat hesitant, I wasn't about to challenge the expert. I accepted the new medication and began to taper off Prozac.

I began reading about bipolar disorder, revisiting the book *Touched with Fire: Manic-Depressive Illness and the Artistic Temperament*, by Kay Redfield Jamison, one of the foremost authorities on bipolar illness. I'd read her first book, *An Unquiet Mind*, because it was recommended by my therapist during my 2014 depression. Because I connected to it on a deep level, I began reading her other books. *Touched with Fire* was intriguing to me as an artist at that time, though I didn't consider that I, too, might be bipolar.

I learned that some of my favorite writers, including Virginia Woolf, Mark Twain, and Edgar Allan Poe, had likely suffered from the illness. Jamison argues that writers and artists show a disproportionate rate of depression and bipolar disorder, something that felt true to my experience. One of the passages that struck me the most explained how artists are more in rhythm with the "pulse of life" and the natural world. We're able to revel in the in-betweenness of things—"brinks, borders, and edges of nature"—make sense of opposite states, and find connections between unlikely things. Many things started to come together in my mind. My obsession with twilight, borders, and transcendence seemed to have an explanation. Writing poetry to give shape to my never-ending questions felt almost like a logical conclusion.

MARCUS CAME TO visit me in Princeton in February. He still hadn't moved in with me like we had planned, but he had quit his job and was in the process of relocating. I was getting tired of him not having a plan to move or get a job. I was resentful that I worked so hard while he just puttered about. I was losing attraction to him because he just went to the gym and sat around all day doing god knows what on his laptop. I asked him to leave but then took it back on the way to the airport because of his haranguing. After a few stormy weeks between us, he returned to Chicago and I left for a literary festival in Mexico City. When I returned to New Jersey, I went to my doctor for a routine checkup. My period was late, which didn't worry me much because it had been irregular for the past few months. They took a pregnancy test as a matter of protocol.

A few minutes later, the nurse returned to the examination room smiling and said, "Congratulations." Having spent my entire adult life avoiding pregnancy, for a second I thought she meant, *Congratulations, you're* not *pregnant.* I soon realized that was not the case. She must have assumed that, at my age, this was good news.

And maybe it was. Or could have been. Though it was not planned, I had to admit that I had been careless with contraception, and I knew that I did want children at some point. I was in my thirties and had a partner and career, after all. Why *wouldn't* I do this?

I called Marcus immediately and told him the news. "You know how I've gained a little bit of weight? It's because I'm pregnant!" I said and laughed. "Can you believe it?"

Marcus didn't share my enthusiasm. "Are you serious? Oh my God," he said and paused for a long time. "I told you to take the morning-after pill."

My joy slowly deflated. "I know we didn't plan on this, but aren't you excited?"

"I don't know what to feel."

MARCUS CAME BACK to New Jersey so we could make a decision together. We considered our options, how we were going to make it all work. He was worried because he wasn't where he wanted to be in his career. Feeling that his last job, an administrative position at a hospital, had been menial, he'd quit. He wanted to go back to school to study neuroscience, although he had done nothing to make this happen. He was thirty-one with a bachelor's degree and an as-yet unestablished career. Up to that point, what his jobs had had in common was that each bore no relation to the previous job and would bear no relation to its successor. He was a man with absolutely no plan.

Marcus's lack of direction and ambition made me nervous from the beginning of our relationship, especially since my career was taking off, but I felt that he had potential, and that the potential was reason enough for everything to work out. I didn't want him to depend on me financially and worried that he would grow to resent me for my success. Typically, a lack of career was a deal breaker for me. I had worked too hard to settle for a man who didn't have his life together. It wasn't just that, though. His apartment was a dump. I'm so embarrassed to admit that he slept on a mattress on the floor and rarely bought groceries. But if there's something I'm good at, it's repressing my concerns for my romantic partners' shortcomings. I smother the shit out of them with the intoxicating haze of falling in love.

Marcus's apprehension concerned me. Yes, we were in our thirties, but maybe this *was* bad timing. We discussed our future over and over again—living situation, careers, money. I told only a few friends and decided to wait to tell my family.

A few weeks later, Marcus began accusing me of trying to trap him. He felt the situation was my fault. We'd had unprotected sex, but that was a mutual decision, and the following day, I'd decided not to take the morning-after pill. I very stupidly believed that everything would be OK, that if I were to get pregnant, we would make it work. I thought we were in it together. I trusted in something that didn't exist. Though I knew it would be an ordeal, I wanted this child. *Aren't most pregnancies unplanned?* I thought. *Don't people just make it work somehow?* My parents managed to raise the three of us on factory wages, and here I was, a grown-ass woman teaching at an Ivy League university, terrified to have a baby.

All at once, things were bad. And yet, taking stock of my emotions, I realized that I'd been feeling bad even before breaking the news of my pregnancy to Marcus. I couldn't make sense of it. I kept feeling worse and worse. I thought vaguely about the change in my medication. It was obvious that the new pills weren't working, but I was so overwhelmed and confused that I never thought to ask my doctor to change my medication again. Maybe it would just take time for the new meds to kick in, I reasoned. I cried constantly, and I assumed some of it was hormonal; I had something growing inside me, after all. How could I possibly be my normal self? But I also considered that this should be one of the happiest times of my life.

I was still traveling for work, but I was barely able to keep my shit together, a walking disaster. I'd visit schools and encourage teens to be true to themselves and follow their dreams while I was on the brink of a full-fledged meltdown. I struggled through these presentations with tears in my eyes, convinced I was full of shit. I was not the tough feminist writer they thought I was. I was a fraud.

Marcus was the only person who knew how serious it was. I didn't know what to do. *Should I continue this pregnancy even though I'm losing my fucking mind?* I wondered. I was in airports weeping behind my sunglasses, hoping no one would notice. I sobbed in hotel rooms. I wandered cities in a state of panic. My body was taut with anxiety, like a clock wound too tight. One day as I drove to my apartment in New Jersey, I let out a wail so loud and primitive that it terrified me. My body had never made a noise like that. I had experienced depression many times before, but this was different. The despair was beyond anything I'd ever known, so inconceivable that even now as I write this I'm unnerved.

Despite wanting to kill myself, I continued teaching. Once a week I taught my students young adult fiction. I discussed the mechanics of storytelling in multicultural coming-of-age stories while I pretended that everything was fantastic, because there was no way I was going to fuck up my fellowship. I was a girl from Cicero who had gotten her ass to Princeton. I did my absolute best to be a professor worthy of these brilliant kids. I suppose my Mexican work ethic was stronger than my illness. If my parents could work in factories every day, I could teach a class.

In addition to my existing worries, I began to obsess about my medication. I knew that Prozac, having been on the market for so long, had been extensively studied and was relatively safe during pregnancy, but I had no idea if Abilify was. From what I could gather on the internet, it was unknown whether it could cause fetal harm, and should be used only if the potential benefits outweighed the potential risks. All websites said to consult a doctor.

I asked my psychiatrist over and over again if it was OK for me to take Abilify. She insisted it was fine, but I wasn't convinced. I told her I was considering an abortion, and she shook her head. In her thick Russian accent, she responded, "Abortion always bad." I didn't know that a doctor was allowed to say that, but I didn't challenge her. In my sad and bewildered state, I simply agreed and left. I don't know what I expected to hear from this doctor who, when I told her my sex drive was low, recommended that I just "lie there" because men's egos are fragile.

What if she was wrong and the medication hurt the fetus? What if it caused birth defects? What if my child had a horrible life fraught with pain and it was all my fault? I agonized over having an abortion. Marcus said that the decision was up to me, but I wanted to be absolutely certain, and I was torn.

I made an appointment at Planned Parenthood. I didn't know if I could survive the pregnancy, so aborting it felt like the best— and only—decision. I was falling apart in every way possible; I felt like I was being held together with only string. I tried my best to eat, but I was struggling, and I knew that whatever I could manage wasn't anywhere near enough to nourish a baby. I slept too much and cried until I thought I would run out of tears. One day I was so anxious and distracted that I rear-ended a car. Thankfully, there was no damage to the other car and the driver let it go, but it startled me. I knew I couldn't keep going like this.

I drove myself to the clinic, because to my mind, I had no one to take me. I didn't have many friends in Jersey. Jen, my best friend, lived about forty-five minutes away in Staten Island, but I didn't want to bother her. I had other friends in Manhattan and Brooklyn, but reaching out to them didn't even cross my mind. I'd always been too proud to ask for help. It's one of my fatal flaws. I could be dying of thirst in the desert and be too embarrassed to ask anyone for a sip of water. I told Jen through text that I was in the Planned Parenthood waiting room. She was upset that I hadn't told her sooner and offered to drive over right that second.

I sat in the examination room after the ultrasound. A sudden hope pulsed inside me. *I can do this,* I said to myself. Despite all the turmoil I was in, I wanted the baby. I told the nurse that I had decided against the procedure. She asked me if I wanted the ultrasound picture and I said yes. The front desk gave me a refund, and I drove back home somewhat relieved. I placed the fuzzy outline of my future child on my altar.

The relief didn't last, however. My depression worsened immediately after. Though I'd chosen to continue the pregnancy, I hadn't figured out how to fix my brain. Every waking moment felt like penance. All I wanted to do was sleep and disappear. Through my unraveling, I continued to teach and to travel. I would summon all the strength I had to make it through a class or panel, and once it was over, I would go back home or to my hotel room and lose it. I did the best I could, because even though I was in a state of abject misery, a part of me still valued my work, and I clung to that.

I made an appointment with an ob-gyn for an ultrasound. I was over two months pregnant. I didn't tell the doctor about my depression. *It will pass*, I kept telling myself. *You will get through this*. I'd never pretended so hard to be fine. My denial about the state of my mental health was otherworldly. I didn't even tell her about the new medication I was on. I'm not sure why. So much of that time is a blur, which I later learned is a function of depression. Your mind sometimes erases pain, because it's too much to remember. I should be grateful for that. Sometimes I wish it would erase entire months, years, people.

But I will never forget the image on the screen. I saw it move. *That's my baby*, I thought to myself as I watched the nebulous little creature. *She's mine. She exists.*

I always assumed it was a "she." I thought my body was trying to tell me something. I planned to name her Clara, after my paternal grandmother, one of my favorite people in the world. Sometimes I spoke to her and told her everything was going to be all right. I put the new ultrasound picture on my fridge.

I THOUGHT ABOUT killing myself often. That was one way to solve all my problems, to end both me and the pregnancy. It would be great for my book sales, I joked with myself. *Young Latina Writer Commits Suicide, Novel Returns to the New York Times Bestseller List*. But, of course, I thought about Marcus and my family. How could I do that to them? What kind of person would I be? My mom would never recover from it, that I knew for certain. In escaping a life I could no longer bear, I would be destroying several others. In some ways my guilt is what kept me alive.

One night I sobbed on the phone as I spoke to Marcus. I told him I didn't know how I was going to survive this. Part of it was the state of my mental health, but I also knew I didn't have his support. He never once told me he wanted this child. He said he was worried about me and suggested I get an abortion. I told him it was too late. I was almost three months pregnant at that point and I knew that medically I could, but how would I survive that emotionally? "You're not getting any better, and this is becoming a life-or-death situation." He offered to fly out that very night. I told him not to but agreed to make an appointment.

I ASSUMED IT was a good clinic because it was called Princeton Women's Services. As my friend later joked, I thought I was having an "Ivy League abortion."

Far from prestigious, the clinic was ancient, and the waiting room was full of crestfallen couples. A mother reassured her teen daughter accompanied by her boyfriend that the procedure was no big deal. The young woman was wearing fuzzy house slippers, and her party of three was oddly calm. I was the only woman in the waiting room who was there alone.

My doctor was an older man, probably in his seventies. I don't even remember his name. What I do remember is that he had stains on his button-down shirt, and that at one point, while a fellow patient and I were waiting in another area inside, we saw him dozing off in a chair in the room across from us. I'm a strong believer in naps, but that seemed straight-up bizarre. I didn't feel right about the clinic, wished I had gone back to Planned Parenthood, but I couldn't get another appointment for weeks, and I needed to get this done as soon as possible.

The doctor wanted to know how old I was. When I said I was thirty-four he asked me if I was sure about the abortion, told me that it was a good time to have a baby. *Yes, it's a great time for a baby,* I thought, *when you're not suicidal.* There was no way to convey to this man that this was the worst I'd ever felt in my life, that if I didn't have this abortion, I would probably end up killing myself. Not only that, but I had also already taken a pill to make my cervix contract, and the thought of worrying about another medication hurting the fetus was too much to endure. I just wanted to get it over with.

Because I had driven myself to the clinic, I could not be sedated—I learned that at my Planned Parenthood appointment—but even if I hadn't driven, there was a sign at the front desk that stated they didn't offer it, which I found alarming.

I was fully conscious for the entire procedure. I didn't even have Xanax or anything close. Had I thought it through, I would have fished out some old antianxiety pills from under my bathroom sink. I don't know how to describe the pain. I've been a writer for most of my life, and words fail me here. I will never be able to articulate what it feels like having a piece of yourself pulled from you. A piece you loved and named.

Though I put on my headphones, I still heard the machine. I

don't remember the songs I played, only that they were loud. What kind of music would be appropriate for the occasion? After it was over, I saw the glass container of the remains. I was angry that they had been so careless in leaving it where I'd see it, and when I pointed it out to the nurse, she looked embarrassed and covered it with a paper sheet. But it was too late. The image was seared into my memory.

I didn't have any food at home, since going to the grocery store at that time in my life was a heroic act—I was mostly subsisting on cereal—so on my way back to my apartment, I stopped for a burger at a fast-food restaurant. I texted the people who knew about my appointment that I was OK. It was the saddest lunch in the history of lunches.

When I tell people this part of the story, they stare at me in disbelief, mouths agape.

I taught my fiction class that evening.

I WILL BE forever pro-choice. Perhaps it's more accurate to say that I believe in reproductive freedom and justice. I think everyone has the right to bodily autonomy and that we're all entitled to comprehensive health care. Abortions should be safe and accessible, and if women choose to have children, they should be able to raise them in a safe and healthy environment.

But I will never pretend that my abortion was easy. It was, without a doubt, the worst experience of my life. However, if I could go back in time and do it all over again, I would. I believe the procedure saved me. I do wish, though, that I had gotten a proper Ivy League abortion. Summa cum laude and Phi Beta Kappa. The works. That clinic was a fucking dump.

You don't hear much about the difficult aftermath of abortion among progressives. Part of this, I suspect, is out of fear of feeding antichoice sentiment. Those "pro-life" people are fucking nuts and I totally understand not wanting to add fuel to their fire. I have a mental illness and I have no qualms about calling these people crazy. Cuckoo fucking bananas. I've seen them with my own eyes and their hysteria scares me to my core. But I think those of us who have struggled with this experience need to feel like we're not alone. Where can we possibly talk about this without being pelted with stones? This is tricky because most people have a hard time understanding nuanced situations. It's always: Abortion! Thumbs-up or thumbs-down?

I burned both ultrasound pictures the day after. I wanted no physical evidence that the pregnancy had ever happened, even though I knew I would live with it forever.

I DON'T REMEMBER what Marcus said to me during that time. Did he try to console me? Did he offer to fly out again? I think that it's telling that I've forgotten all our conversations.

Less than a week after the procedure, I shook and sobbed on my couch and knew I couldn't survive without immediate intervention. I canceled my class that week and several upcoming events and trips, and checked myself into a psychiatric hospital. Before I left, I called my brothers and told them what was happening. I didn't want to tell my mom because I knew she would be in distress, so I made up a story about a last-minute trip abroad. I changed my mind almost immediately, because I knew I couldn't keep up the lie. I told her that I was checking myself into a psych ward. I've always been a shitty liar, so I didn't even try. She offered to take the next flight to New Jersey, but I refused, assured her I was fine.

I wasn't.

It had been nineteen years since I'd last been in a psych ward. Most of it was the same—lots of group therapy. No shoelaces, phones, or razors allowed. Terrible food that could make a person more suicidal. I roomed with a young Puerto Rican woman who was struggling with drug addiction. Lots of patients wore sweats or pajamas. I couldn't bring myself to do it, because as depressed as I was, I was still holding on to my last shred of dignity. I got dressed and applied my makeup every day, even though everything felt so utterly pointless.

The best part of the experience was "horse therapy." On a cold and rainy afternoon, a woman led us in a game of kickball with a pair of horses. Whenever we kicked the ball, we would pull the horses to the bases with us. It made no sense, but I adore horses, so much that I have two tattooed on my right arm. Their mere presence gave me a sliver of peace.

My psychiatrist at the hospital, a young and terse Middle Eastern woman, changed my medication again, and confirmed that my previous psychiatrist was wrong about Abilify being safe for the fetus. "You made the right choice," she assured me, and I sat there both furious and confused.

Marcus returned to New Jersey. He stayed in my apartment

and visited me every day at the hospital. Everyone assumed he was my husband, and something about that made me feel hopeful. Maybe he would be if I survived this.

I was in the hospital for only a week because I insisted they let me out in time for a Skype interview I had scheduled with a university for a teaching position. A few hours after I got out of the hospital, I tried to convince a committee of professors that they should hire me to teach poetry.

I didn't get the job. (Cue sad trombone.)

I'm not sure how helpful the hospital was, because I was still distraught, but at least they kept me from offing myself. I started an outpatient program the next day, which meant more group therapy. I continued to learn about healthy ways to cope with my depression: gratitude journals, exercise, adult coloring books (?), healthy sleeping habits, and self-compassion, all of which felt pointless.

Marcus left after a few days. I'm not even sure why, because it's not like he had a job to return to. Now I wonder why he didn't just move in with me, but at the time I just accepted it. I was so broken, nothing made sense to me.

THE WORST PART of the depression, besides wanting to die, is that it took away my personality. I wasn't living—I was barely surviving, aguantando. I didn't care about anything—except teaching, I suppose, because I kept doing it. And that alone required every single ounce of strength I could summon. I couldn't read or write for pleasure. I didn't crack any jokes and nothing made me laugh, which is unsettling because I'm a clown at heart. It's my go-to coping mechanism; I can find the humor in a tube sock. I'm also known among my friends and family for my voracious appetite, but in this exquisite haze, everything tasted like sand, and I ate only to stay alive. My sex drive was nonexistent, dried up like an abandoned well. Normally my libido is so high that it's a nuisance, but the depression had burrowed itself so deep inside me I thought it was forever extinguished. I couldn't even picture having sex again, the act completely inconceivable. And I wasn't about to take Dr. Petrov's advice and "just lie there" for anybody. My Buddhist faith wavered through all this, too. I felt betrayed by it. Before, I was able to find meaning in my suffering, but the suffering this time meant nothing to me.

The only positive outlet that I had was running, and, remarkably, I kept at it. I ran five miles several times a week, mostly because Marcus insisted and scolded me when I didn't. He was right to encourage me, as it did make me feel better, but it was far from a cure. I often wept as I ran. Sometimes I wanted to throw myself into a ditch. I wished the earth would open up and swallow me whole. "Don't die, Erika," I would tell myself aloud. "Please don't die." One afternoon I saw a fox and it was so striking it gave me a glimmer of faith. I remembered that even in misery there is beauty. I suppose that's how we survive.

During one of my group therapy sessions, we were tasked with choosing a song to play. I chose Nina Simone's rendition of "Here Comes the Sun." The song played and I began to sob uncontrollably. It just wasn't true. The sun was already there and I hated it. I hated being alive. It wasn't fair to have to exist. The others in the class looked worried for me, and I drove home playing the song on repeat and crying so hard I could hardly see the road.

As if I didn't have enough to worry about, acne took over my face. (Is there an uglier word in the English language? The answer is no.) It had started at the beginning of the year and kept getting worse. It was red, angry, and painful. I had struggled with my skin on and off since I was thirteen, but this was the most severe it had ever been. Nothing made it better, no matter how much money I spent on products or how many dermatologists I saw. I tried my best to cover it with makeup, but it was futile. I was in a constant state of humiliation and hated looking in the mirror. I didn't want anyone to even glance in my direction. It was as if whatever turmoil I had inside me was manifesting itself on my face in the most embarrassing way possible. I was so desperate that I considered going on Accutane, which is funny because one of the possible side effects is suicidal thoughts.

Roughly one month after my abortion, I was staring down Mother's Day. It was one of the worst days of my life. My friend Jackson had recently moved to Brooklyn, so they took the train to Princeton that weekend to console me after I told them what had happened. When I'd met Jackson in Chicago in 2015, we were very different people. I was on the verge of getting married and they had not yet transitioned.

They stayed the weekend and there were moments I almost felt like myself again. Jackson made me the best vegetable curry I've ever had. It was reassuring to eat real food again. I even managed to laugh a few times. But on Sunday morning after they left, I couldn't stop crying. I spent almost the entire day on my couch. I called a suicide hotline, but no one answered, which I didn't know was a thing. At one point I got on my knees sobbing and screaming, "Somebody please help me." I still don't know who or what I was begging—I don't believe in an interventionist God—but that's how dire it was.

MY MIND BRANCHED out into the darkest places during those weeks after Mother's Day. I convinced myself I was damaged beyond repair after the abortion and would never have children. Part of this worry stemmed from the fact that I had bled for a month after the procedure. Despite having a checkup in which everything appeared to be normal, I was certain that my life was ruined.

One weekend, Jen took me to a Hindu ashram in upstate New York to help with my healing process. While there, I meditated and begged the universe to deliver me from this never-ending horror. That afternoon, as we sat in the cafeteria eating a too-healthy vegan lunch, I saw a biracial toddler waddle between tables. He was brown and curly haired, just like I imagined my child to be. The tears poured out of my eyes against my will. I tried to compose myself, but Jen insisted I let the grief work its way out. I wondered if it ever could.

· · ·

I MADE A brief trip to Chicago for Memorial Day weekend. I stayed only a few days because I was still in my outpatient program. My family knew about the hospitalization, of course, but they didn't know about the abortion. It's not that I was ashamed of it, but I didn't want them to hurt with me. It was also difficult for me to talk about it. I couldn't even discuss it in group therapy, and I had concluded I would never be able to write about it. I couldn't imagine the world knowing about the worst moment of my life.

The night I arrived, Marcus and I got tacos, and when we returned to the lot, his car was gone. A man on the street told us it had been towed. Marcus hardly spoke as we tracked down his car on the north side of the city in an Uber. It took hours to get it back, and because he was still fuming, I left him alone. As we drove back to his place I thought about killing myself again. I eventually broke our long, taut silence and said, "If I don't make it, can you please make sure Tom gets Simone?" That was one of my top worries about dying. I wanted my cat to have a good home if I were gone, and I felt that my ex-husband would be the best choice. He had loved her so much and was devastated when I kept her in the divorce.

Marcus said he couldn't believe that I had made the moment about me. He bitched me out as he gripped the steering wheel and looked straight ahead. "If you kill yourself, I will cut off Simone's tail," he said. I was so afraid I said nothing, my body a tight braid.

I spent those few days trying to appear halfway normal around my family, but I wasn't very convincing. We typically show love by trolling each other, and I didn't have it in me this time. I was quiet and distracted instead of talking my usual shit. I worried about what my niece and nephew would think. They were eleven and fourteen at the time, and I didn't want them to worry about their mentally ill aunt. At one point I turned to my brother and asked, "Do the kids know about . . ." Then I pointed my finger to my head and made circles, the universal cartoon sign for crazy. He nodded and we all laughed.

IN LATE MAY, I had a panel at a conference in New York, and the morning before my trip, I planned to take out all my savings from the bank to leave for my family before I committed suicide. It was hot and I couldn't stand being alive any longer. The sun on my skin oppressed me. I was not meant to exist on this earth, I concluded.

I called Marcus and told him I was done. "You can't do this to me," he said. "What about everything you promised? What about our life together? What about everything you said about having a family with me one day?"

So instead of emptying my savings and killing myself, I made myself board the train and did the panel the next morning. This was something I would typically enjoy—staying in a beautiful hotel and discussing my work with other writers in New York—but this time I was imploding and could hardly form words. I don't remember much of the panel—I hope I was somewhat coherent—but I do know I discussed what it was like to be the daughter of immigrants. During the book signing afterward, many young women gushed about my novel, told me it was life-changing, that they had never felt so seen, and as I sat there with a smile so fake it hurt, I wondered what it would mean to them if I ended my life.

MY MOM VISITED me in Jersey for my birthday in early June. The plan was that she'd stay for two weeks, then I would return to Chicago with her as soon as I finished my outpatient program. I reverted to being a child during her time in New Jersey. I was so useless that she took care of me like I was a baby—cooking and cleaning and making sure I ate. She even slept in my bed.

On the morning of my birthday, I paced my apartment and cried. My mom didn't know what to do. She tried to reason with me, told me I'd be OK, but I didn't believe her. I was supposed to read a poem I had written for the Phi Beta Kappa graduation ceremony at Princeton at eight a.m. I was inconsolable, but there was no way I could miss it, so I dried my swollen eyes and muscled through again. I read my poem in front of hundreds of people in a beautiful auditorium and they were none the wiser.

I still hadn't told my family about the abortion. Only Marcus and a few friends knew at that point. I kept it sealed inside me because telling them would somehow make it more true. I also feared how they would react given their faith and our culture. But after dinner one day, I sat at the kitchen table and the truth pounded inside me, pushing its way out. I couldn't look at my mom when I said it. Later that night I called my brothers and told them, too. My mom said she'd tell my dad in person. No one judged me, and I should have known that they wouldn't.

One afternoon, my mom and I ended up praying in an empty Catholic church close to my apartment. I kneeled and sobbed while my mom rubbed my back. I hadn't been Catholic since the age of twelve, but here I was groveling before Jesus again. Desperation makes us do such strange things. A woman came in and put her hand on my shoulder and told me everything was going to be OK. I wanted to believe her, but I didn't. When we got back home, I said to my mom, "Por favor, déjenme ir." In my diseased mind, I thought I'd somehow get my family's blessing to kill myself. Panicked, my mom called my older brother. "I don't want to do this anymore," I told him.

"That's not really an option," he replied, and told us we had to call an ambulance.

AFTER MANY HOURS in the ER, I was back in the psych ward, a nicer one this time. The food was marginally less disgusting and the facility was cleaner and more up-to-date. My roommate was an old white woman whose husband had recently died. When she asked me why I was crying in my bed, I hesitated to tell her about the abortion. Because of her age, I feared she would judge me, and I was too fragile to defend myself. But she didn't. She told me she was sorry.

Marcus flew in from Chicago again, and he and my mom visited me the days I was allowed visitors. Soon after, my little brother came too. I hated that they had to see me like this, all red-eyed, gaunt, and mute. I didn't talk much, and when I did, every word was slow and drawn out. Depression had even changed the way I spoke.

A few days into my stay, I heard two older white women discussing electroconvulsive therapy. They had received the procedure many years before and were in the hospital for a "tune-up" of sorts. Intrigued, I asked them more about it. I knew nothing beyond what I had seen in *One Flew over the Cuckoo's Nest*, which I figured was outdated. Both women told me it was the best decision to treat their depression, and that afterward, they no longer required medication. They were there because it had worn off after many years. I would have agreed to anything at that point. *Crack open my skull and poke my brain with sticks? YES, PLEASE.* I read two pamphlets over and over. In one of them, a poorly drawn sad man gets his brain zapped, then becomes a poorly drawn happy man. I found it mildly amusing. *Please, God/Buddha/Universe, let me become Mr. Happy Man.* The other pamphlet explicitly referenced *One Flew over the Cuckoo's Nest*, stating that the procedure in the movie "bears no resemblance to modern ECT, which is neither painful nor punishment." It also referred to depression as "melancholia," which pleased the old-timey poet inside me. I've long been fascinated by the ancient Greek and Roman concept of "the humors," the system of medicine that posited bodily fluids determined one's temperament. I most definitely would have been diagnosed with excessive black bile, which was believed to cause depression. The word "melancholy," in fact, is derived from the Greek word for "black bile," a disgusting and precise description.

I asked my new psychiatrist, another Russian, about ECT the following afternoon. He had already put me back on Prozac like I'd asked him to, and he quickly agreed that ECT would also be a good course of treatment for me. It's usually used only in worst-case scenarios, once all other options have been exhausted, and that seemed to describe me. Under general anesthesia, small electric currents would be passed through my brain to trigger a seizure, which would change my brain's chemistry. I began treatment the next morning.

The procedure was painless. Every other day, I'd wake up from ECT feeling groggy and then sleep it off. That was the worst of it, really. The results were supposed to be quick, but nothing was quick enough for me. I still brainstormed ways of killing myself in the hospital. One idea was to fashion a long-sleeved shirt into a noose and hang myself from a closet door. (There weren't any rods, of course, because they knew better.) I did attempt this, but quickly changed my mind and stepped back onto the chair. I hurt my throat in the process and for days I wondered if I had broken something, but I told no one. Another idea was to ask for my concealer from my makeup bag, which the staff kept near the front desk. I took my little bottle of concealer and broke it in the bathroom. I was supposed to return all items I used, but I hoped that the attendant would forget. He did, and I kept the shard of glass under my mattress for days, until I decided to throw it away.

The morning I got out of the hospital was bright and hot, what would normally be considered a beautiful day. This was something I wasn't capable of appreciating, because I felt like it was mocking me. *Fuck you, summer. Fuck you and all your goddamn fecundity.* I had very little energy and was disoriented, likely because of the ECT. All I wanted to do was melt into my couch and watch mindless TV, but Marcus insisted that I go for a run that evening. I complied and changed into my running gear. My mom and I walked to the nearby park, where Marcus had already started running. I wasn't quite ready to begin, so my mom and I sat on a bench for a bit. All the inactivity for those two weeks made me so lethargic—my body felt soft and pliable, like a lump of worn clay. I sat and stared off into space for a while, never once considering that such an insignificant act would change my life.

One of the side effects of the ECT I experienced was memory loss. Memory is already slippery, and when you add depression and electricity pulsing through your brain, things can get extra murky, so it's hard for me to accurately piece together what happened next. I don't know if Marcus and I yelled at each other, but I do know that he was furious, convinced that I wasn't trying to get better. He was so disappointed that he packed his things and left for New York to stay with a friend that night. According to him, I said that I would hurt myself if he left, which I don't remember, and I can't confirm because I've deleted his texts.

He returned later that weekend to break up with me and go home.

MY MOM AND I decided that it was not the time for me to be alone, so we drove to Chicago with my cat in tow. The plan was for me to live with my parents for eight weeks while I began yet another outpatient program and looked into the possibility of more ECT. I saw Marcus a handful of times in the beginning. I lied to my family about where I was because everyone hated him, and the secrecy made me feel like a teenager again. "I want you to stay away from that man," my mom had pleaded after he left me in New Jersey. In

Chicago, Marcus and I talked about getting back together, even though it felt wrong to me. I think I was trying to hold on to a piece of my former life, my former self. My brain still wasn't working right and I was making destructive decisions. In his bedroom one evening he began to cry about the abortion. "We lost a kid," he said with tears in his eyes. He asked me to stay with him that night, but I didn't. And that was the last time I ever saw him.

I was enveloped by my family and friends for two beautiful months. I slept in my childhood bed and spent a lot of time with my parents. My mom kept feeding and spoiling me. Everyone showered me with love and encouragement. I continued to run. My skin cleared up and I no longer felt like a monstrosity. I finished my outpatient program and got another six rounds of ECT at a local hospital.

Though I was improving mentally, I was starting to have bouts of nausea and would throw up whenever I was in a moving car. I insisted I was fine and that it would pass, but my parents took me to the emergency room one night anyway. The doctors there had no clue what was wrong with me. I saw two other doctors after that: one thought it was the Prozac, but didn't articulate why, and the other insisted it was an ear infection. It wasn't until I saw my ECT nurse practitioner again that I learned what was really happening. "I think you have excess serotonin," she said. "Now that the procedure has changed your brain chemistry, your Prozac prescription is too high."

I was dumbfounded. I had spent the majority of my life depressed, feeling like something in my brain was deficient, and now I was being told that I had an excessive amount of the chemical responsible for my emotional well-being. Well, that was a mind-fuck.

"I have too much serotonin!" I told my little brother when he came by our parents' house later that day. "Isn't that nuts?"

"Yeah, I thought it was weird you were laughing at all my jokes," he said, which also made me laugh.

As my departure approached, I began feeling almost normal again. Well, maybe "normal" isn't the right word; if I'm being honest with myself, I don't even know what that is. It was more like magic, as if someone had flipped a switch and I was suddenly fixed. I still can hardly believe it. I thought depression would always be part of my life, but maybe I was wrong. Perhaps I'd created a new reality—perhaps I had to destroy everything to start over, again. *Thank you, science,* I thought and looked at the sky. *Thank you for giving me back to myself.*

When I tell people about the ECT, they often look incredulous. Some are flat-out horrified that I underwent this procedure. "Wow, that seems so extreme," several people have said to me, shuddering. They always want to know if it was painful, and they're surprised when I explain how effortless it was. Despite the bad PR, I have no doubt that it was one of the best decisions of my life.

Modern ECT is a warm, delicate ocean breeze compared to other methods used in the past. Historically, treatments for mental illness included extreme measures such as enemas, vomiting, exorcisms, bloodletting, and lobotomies. Many people were shunned and isolated. Some were even drowned or burned to death. Ancient Romans, Greeks, and Mesopotamians believed that mental illness was a result of demonic possession. Sometimes I wonder what would have happened to me if I'd been born at a different time. Maybe I would have been tried as a witch!

At the height of my depression, I thought I would never write again. I worried that I would have to give up my fellowship and move back home. Most of the time I wondered if I would survive at all. Recently, while going through my journals to mine material for this essay, I found a letter that I don't remember writing. It's not dated or addressed to anyone, but I know I wrote it during my second hospital stay, the time I stepped back onto the chair for reasons not entirely known to me. Fear? Hope? Resilience? Cowardice? Guilt? Love? In the letter I told everyone I was sorry. The end reads: "It's no one's fault. It was me. Only me."

I DROVE BACK to Princeton with my dad and cat in early September. My family and friends worried that I would be alone the last year of my fellowship, but I knew that I would not only survive, I would flourish. I was whole. I was writing. I was capable of joy. I laughed. Food tasted like itself.

I always believed that I felt too much, cursed my sensitivity, but who would I be without it? I wonder now. Through my recovery, I fell in love with life for the first time. I became enchanted beyond belief. I was delighted by the simplest things. I whispered to birds, I thanked trees, I looked up at the sky and felt devastated by its beauty.

My return to writing felt like slowly pulling nails from my body. Writing, that delicious ache, is what has always kept me alive. Words for me are a form of prayer, a kind of reverence. They say *thank you, thank you, thank you.*

I AM NOT YOUR PERFECT
MEXICAN MOM

The final year of my fellowship was remarkable because my depression was finally under control and I was able to work and travel again—a welcome change after the year that had preceded it. All I needed to do was stay alive. I did that and more. I returned to professional spaces that had always humbled and excited me, and I rose to the occasion. When the fellowship ended in June, I was proud of what I accomplished. I said goodbye to Princeton, and I moved back to Chicago.

The year had also been very unsexy, and after settling into my new home—an apartment in my old neighborhood of Bridgeport—and feeling ready to begin my chair position at DePaul University, I believed it was time to find a romantic partner. Not surprisingly, there'd been no prospects in suburban New Jersey, and even when I traveled, I came up empty. I had wandered through Italy, London, Dublin, and many US cities, eyes peeled for some peen, but besides a brief dalliance in Virginia with a man who was much too young for me, I was unsuccessful. My numerous romantic failures had made me incredibly selective, almost unreasonably so. Finding sex as an attractive woman is as easy as diner eggs, but when you're aging and tired of empty encounters with men who don't own bed frames, that shit gets tricky. I was traumatized by my most recent relationship, and there was no way I was going to fall for some loser again. I'd rather be a sexy born-again spinster for the rest of my days.

With deep existential dread, I downloaded the dating apps that I had previously found so loathsome. *Here we go again*—I sighed, shuddered, and made the sign of the cross. During a visit to my family in Mexico that summer, my tía had given me a limpia to help me get rid of the ghosts of penises past. I was ready. Sorta. *Let's do this!*

I often thought of escape routes as soon as I laid eyes on a suitor. It was not that I found them all unattractive, but I knew instantly in my heart of hearts (loin of loins) whether I wanted to sit on someone's face. This is the bare minimum for me. Whenever a friend of mine wavers in her feelings for a gentleman caller, that is my first question: "Do you want to sit on his face?" My philosophy remains that you can't stay with someone you feel "medium" about. You need to love the smell of his scalp, the way he eats his sandwich, you feel me? I myself had tricked my brain into dating men I wasn't really into: "Well, maybe the attraction will grow because he's a nice person!" Bitch, no. It will not.

On my various profiles, I said that I was looking for a funny man of color. Obviously, I wanted someone who was smart and successful. I had a few more nonnegotiable rules for myself: no white dudes (bad for my psyche, spirit, and general well-being), no one broke, and under no circumstances would I consider anyone who did not want children. Lastly, I didn't want to be a mother to a grown man. I had breakfast with an okayish-looking lawyer early in my foray back into dating, and when he invited me back to his place, I was shocked to find he was living in what was ostensibly an elevated dorm room, and that's being generous. After Marcus, that was triggering as hell.

"So what do you think of my apartment?" he asked.

Grimacing, I responded, "Ehhhhh. Welllll . . . it's not great."

He smiled and responded with, "Hey, but at least I have hand soap in the bathroom, right?"

". . ."

He was trying to be funny, but there's no way I was going to date someone who bragged about basic human hygiene. (Just around the corner, we as a people would experience a wake-up call for the importance of handwashing.)

I met one dude downtown for happy hour and he spent the entire date telling me about his keto diet. This motherfucker wouldn't even eat the appetizers! Shortly after that, I had coffee with a human pyramid scheme—think Jean-Ralphio but melanated. I blocked him as he waited for his Uber. Then I went out with a musician who was much too thirsty in the pants, so I said I had to go home to check on my Crockpot and scurried to my car like a rodent.

Most men did not get past the first date, except for a Nigerian American fellow who got four. He was attractive and successful enough, but among other things that gave me pause, he told me that white women were his "kryptonite" right after we had sex.

Also, he told me going down on women grossed him out. Call me old-fashioned, but I wasn't hearing wedding bells in the distance after that.

All of it was exhausting: "Where are you from? What are your go-to restaurants? How often do you wash your sheets? How do you feel about feminism? Who's your favorite Muppet?" Most dates were as pleasurable as eating undercooked rice. I wished that I didn't want a partner or children, but there was a deep and pulsing need inside me. It would have been so much easier if I could be like Samantha from *Sex and the City*, boinking ugly white dudes without a care in the world while drinking thirty-dollar martinis, but no, my aging body was telling me to procreate and shop at Home Depot. Annoying!

I was beginning to worry because I was thirty-five and really wanted to have children in the next few years. Many people assured me that I was still young and had plenty of time. I know they meant well, but damn, that got annoying. "You know who disagrees?" I wanted to scream. "Science!" While I understand that "plenty of time" is subjective, I wasn't a supple twenty-year-old anymore.

I had a clear picture of the kind of man I wanted: masculine but not macho, brilliant in some form, unreasonably funny, and Brown, absolutely Brown. Back when my standards were as low as my serotonin levels, I ignored my intuition and it had bitten me in the ass. That's how I ended up with Marcus, a man who upon waking each morning would eat Tostitos tortilla chips he kept beside his mattress on the floor. I was starting to consider getting ahold of some high-quality sperm if things didn't begin looking up.

It's hard to date men when you hate men. I usually said this in jest on dates just to test the waters. If a date got defensive, it meant that he was incapable of acknowledging his privilege, and I knew it wouldn't work. I wasn't about to argue with someone about the history of humankind and my own lived experience. Each day I looked at my dating apps in disgust. So many unflattering car selfies and "laid-back guys" who liked to "have fun." I'd delete the apps periodically and convince myself I'd have a meet-cute in a supermarket like a fucking sap in a rom-com. Then I would download them again, because I was a mammal with needs.

Late in the summer I started corresponding with a promising suitor on OkCupid. He was a divorced dad of two who had just bought a house on the north side of the city. What charmed me about him was the way he talked about his kids. He was clearly enamored with them and took his role as father very seriously. When he told me he was working on a rap album that he would give to his kids when they were adults, goddamn it, that really did it for me. A grown man with a good job and a house who is an involved and enthusiastic father? Well, fuck. Color me impressed. I had seen some shit out there, and these qualities combined were a rarity. Also, he was hilarious. He said he used to do stand-up, which would normally make me hesitate because yikes, but his texts always made me giggle. I agreed to go to dinner with him.

As soon as I saw Will, my heart fluttered like a kite stuck in a tree during a tornado. He had kind brown eyes and his beard was thick and luxurious; a beautiful Brown man with a sexy-dork vibe. Imagine Jason Mantzoukas but thicker. I knew he was biracial from his profile—Black and Italian—but he looked like he might be Indian or Middle Eastern, so he probably experienced racism on a few different fronts, which he later confirmed. Either way, hot as fuck. You get my point.

At that time I rarely got nervous on dates, because they were so low stakes for me. I usually knew when a person didn't have any potential as a partner, so I did not care about impressing them. But it was different with Will. He had me laughing so hard that my face hurt. I was howling, frightening the passersby. His general irreverence toward the world delighted me. We had the most absurd conversations right from the start. Twenty minutes in, I told him the Sánchez family lore about my grandmother's cat who was a suspected rapist. That made him cackle, which quickly became one of my favorite sounds. Also, he had Big Dad Energy. Swoon.

After dinner we walked to a few bars and kept talking and laughing. It was a classic Chicago summer night—the cicadas screaming, music blaring from passing cars, the air pulsing with possibility. Everyone seemed happy, including us.

We didn't want to go home, but after over five hours together, it was very late, and Will had to get to work early. I wanted very much to sit on his lovely hirsute face. As we waited to cross the street, he kissed me and it felt like the big bang in my chest. I looked up at him and said, "I like you." "I like you, too," he responded.

He made my insides all hot and quivery, and I couldn't hide it.

As I drove home smiling, I thought to myself, *I have found my future husband.*

I *for real* deleted my dating apps a day or two later, that's how certain I was that we would die of old age together at the same exact time, holding hands and recounting our love like the Brown *Notebook*. I texted friends and told them I'd met the man I would marry. I may have seemed delusional, and I had said some out-landish things in the past, but I was so sure that we were meant to be together that I couldn't help myself. I would move into his house. I would be a loving stepmom to his kids. We would have a baby together. Of course, I told him none of this so he wouldn't think I was touched in the head.

On our second date, Will invited me to his house. He made me a fire in his backyard and we sat there for hours smoking weed and laughing. He was enchanted by my foul mouth. He was equally crass. It turned out we were both epic shit-talkers. I tried to be coy and resisted having sex at first, out of an underlying fear of getting ghosted. What if I was reading the situation wrong? I worried.

Well, my sorry attempt at prudence ended soon after he played "Pony" by Ginuwine, because I am but a mere mortal.

Within a few weeks, I met his kids, his ex-wife, and his friends. I was both relieved and stunned by the healthy co-parenting rela-tionship he had with his ex. Four years after their divorce, there was no animosity between them. She had moved on with a new partner and the kids split their time evenly between both house-holds and were happy and well-adjusted. Their mom and I had an immediate respect for each other, and I genuinely liked her. I had never seen a blended family that functioned like that. I thought that was some shit you'd see on TV. Will was a for-real grown-up, and that gave me palpitations.

He was also very clearly a feminist without ever calling himself one. He didn't make it about himself and thereby cancel it out. I saw it in the way he treated me, his daughter, his ex-wife, and every other woman he interacted with.

Will and I were together several days a week, and I fell in love with him a little more every time I was with him. He was the first person who made me feel seen. He appreciated everything about me and didn't just pick things à la carte. He wasn't afraid of my too-muchness. He thought I was hilarious and brilliant and beautiful. And, as a proper man from Atlanta, he venerated my booty.

We continued making fires in his backyard. We smoked joints and listened to rap while his dumb white pit bull chased rats.

Dear reader, how do I tell a love story without making you barf? I promise to try: He gave me a boner of the heart. I loved him like I loved writing. The way I loved the sky's unreasonable colors at dusk. The sound of thawing snow in March. The ache of a beautiful poem. A greasy street taco at three a.m. The clopping of a horse in the distance. The smell of wet earth after a thunderstorm. A love so deep it terrified me in its boundlessness. With him, I was a more audacious version of myself. It was gross.

I moved in with Will after five months, though I essentially lived there soon after we met. I was laughing all day, every day. It was like living with Richard Pryor without all the trauma.

We thought 2020 was a year of limitless potential (ha!). The play adaptation of *I Am Not Your Perfect Mexican Daughter* premiered at Steppenwolf Theatre in Chicago in February. Opening night was one of the most emotional nights of my entire life. I adored the adaptation. Everyone who worked on the play was brilliant. My entire family and most of my friends were there. I laughed, I cried, I yelled at some white ladies on the street. (A story for a different time!) After the performance, most of the cast and crew joined our friends and family at our house and we partied until two a.m. It was legendary.

THEN CAME THE plague of biblical proportions.

At first we approached it with a cautious hope, like I imagine many people did. There was so much we didn't know, and we assumed that the crisis would be short-lived. We sheltered in place and tried to make the most of the situation. The kids, the girl seven and the boy eight, were bored as fuck, so we found ways to entertain them. Will dressed up in a blond wig, hat, and sunglasses and called himself Professor Sausage. For some mysterious reason, he showed them a video of how hot dogs were made. One day I dressed in a long skirt, feathered boa, and a kerchief on my head and called myself Old Lady McGonigal. She was the guest expert on manners and kindness and had an egregious British accent.

Will also coached me on stand-up and I performed a short set for my friends and family through Zoom while wearing running shorts, socks and slides, and a fake fur coat. I made fun of my transmutation into a señora. Basically, one day you're doing club drugs with drag queens and the next you're being passive-aggressive to your pets.

Let's make the most of this pandemic, we thought. *What else can we fucking do?*

Then I got pregnant. At last, the baby I'd been dreaming up for years! Will and I were elated despite basically everything. I reveled in the thought of this little human. I was already living in the future: a Frappuccino-colored child with big loose curls and a delightful squeal. At ease with the world and free in ways I was not.

My belly grew with the spread of the virus. Pregnancy was concurrently ordinary and extraordinary. I was making an actual human with my body, like women had done for millennia. It's a real mindfuck, let me tell you. Within a few weeks we learned that the baby was a girl. It was what I wanted but was afraid to admit to myself and others. You're supposed to say you don't care, as long as they're healthy. But I cared. I cared a lot.

I wanted to raise a girl to be defiant and brilliant and funny. I wanted a friend, someone who trusted me with the truth even when it hurt. I wanted to raise someone to love every part of herself, to be who she was without any hesitation. *You're a different gender than we thought? Cool. Let's go shopping. You want to convert to a religion that worships garden gnomes? OK, as long as you don't oppress anyone! You want to change your name to Wizard Cat Sánchez? I don't really get it, but I guess. You want to move to Mozambique? Great, I'll visit you and bring you Milagro tortillas.*

I wanted to give my daughter the permission that no one had given me. And I knew that one of the best things I had already done for her was choose her father.

Pregnant, I could no longer cloud my mind with unreasonable amounts of weed, so I had to come to terms with our new reality. Then came the nausea, headaches, and exhaustion. By month five or so, I began to hear the baby cry inside me in the middle of the night. Toward my due date, I also started to hear something that was between a groan and a croak. It scared me a bit, but I was mostly amused. I never woke Will to listen. I would wait for it to subside and go back to sleep.

We became listless and scared. The death toll grew. We watched footage of Trump in disgust. We yelled at the TV. People died as we sat useless in our living room. Black men and women were murdered by police so frequently over these past few years that there were times we began to conflate the ways in which they died. *Was he the one who . . . ? Was she the one who . . . ? Didn't they . . . ? His daughter in the car . . . His neck . . . A Wendy's parking lot . . . She was asleep. . . . He yelled for his mother. . . .*

Will and I had countless conversations about whiteness and privilege, about our fears about raising our blended Brown family in a white supremacy, in a country where millions of people revered a fascist. *What is white culture?* we wondered. A disease of the psyche. A gluttony of the spirit. A failure of the imagination. We concluded that whiteness was an ideology that valued appearances, charades, secrecy, dishonesty, and dominance. To be white is to be at the center of it all and still want more.

I worried for the girl forming inside me. What would the world look like as she grew? Though our family was enduring the pandemic relatively unscathed, Will and I were in a constant state of rage and trepidation. What would it mean if Trump got reelected? How would we raise these racially ambiguous children? We joked about me giving birth to our daughter in Canada. An anchor baby to escape racist whites.

We watched HGTV, we read books, we jump-roped, we painted the house, we vogued, we rapped, we rearranged furniture, we complained, we felt guilty, we donated, we remodeled the base-ment, we cried, we cooked weird shit, we bought stupid shit, we made art, we created characters, we saw family in our yard, we made bread like every other asshole. The soundtrack to the year included the constant barrage of pharmaceutical commercials: *Side effects may include suicidal thoughts, hotness of the ears, sweaty neck syndrome, butt teeth, delusions of grandeur, diarrhea, heart palpitations, existential despair, acne, and death.*

In May, Will proposed to me in the very yard where we fell in love. I was wearing sweatpants, a ratty Keith Haring T-shirt, no bra, no makeup. Obviously, I'd had no idea it was coming. We had talked about getting married, but I assumed he hadn't bought a ring during quarantine. One warm night he reached inside our herb planter and produced a box with a beautiful ring. Of course I said yes.

A few months later we got married in the same place, in front of our tomato plants. We wanted to be married despite the pan-demic. Our friend Miguel officiated because he was already or-dained online and badda-bing-badda-boom! We had only two other people in attendance—my little brother and Will's best friend. We ate our favorite deep-dish pizza. It was silly and fun and sweet.

THROUGHOUT QUARANTINE WE thought about what to name our daughter. I wanted a name that was proud and rare, maybe even defiant. We wanted her name to represent the time in history and her mixed identity. Will suggested Sojourner and it made me gasp. Holy shit, what a name, I thought. Sojourner Truth. *Ain't I a Woman?* A traveler. A brilliant abolitionist. A woman who belongs to no one. A woman who named herself. How could you ever disrespect a Sojourner? How could a man expect subservience from a woman like that? Her name says *I dare you to.*

I added Inés, after Sor Juana Inés de la Cruz, because I wanted her to love knowledge and live a thousand lives through books. A learned rebel. A woman of critical thought. Then we hyphenated our last names because I made her in my body and I won't be erased by tradition.

Sojourner Inés, her name as a form of protection.

EVEN AS A YOUNG GIRL, I knew I wanted my life to be my own before I shared it with a child. I couldn't fathom sacrificing my needs and wants to raise children. I didn't want to resent my kids for the life I'd never had. I was going to have that life at any cost. I was going to build it before she came.

I know there are women who succeed no matter what their circumstances are, rising above every obstacle in their paths, but I don't think I would have been one of them. I'm not heroic like that. Thinking about the thousands of children separated at the border from their mothers makes me tremble inside with rage. Our society doesn't truly value motherhood, just the idea of it. Instead, it is openly hostile toward mothers. I had seen cousins, aunts, and classmates have kids in their teens, and the consequences of that stunned me. I wasn't interested in the martyrdom of motherhood. I did not want to suffer like that. Contrary to what many people

think, selfishness had nothing to do with it; it was about staying alive.

SOJOURNER WAS BORN with no complications. The only thing of
note was that she didn't cry when she came out. She looked around
perplexed, as if assessing this bright new world she had just entered. I kept worrying about it and craning my neck to see her
across the delivery room, but the doctors assured me she was fine.
There's a picture Will took shortly after her birth in which she
is smiling, her big black eyes like planets. She looks like some sort
of space creature to me. Her strange expression always makes me
giggle.

I was on maternity leave from my position as the Sor Juana Inés
de la Cruz chair at DePaul. Even with time and resources, parent-
ing had me in a constant frenzy. Keeping a person alive was an
extraordinary amount of work. Babies are hard. Who knew?
Though I was exhausted, I knew how lucky I was. Will and I were
financially secure and he was also given parental leave. Even after
my maternity leave, my job as a professor allowed me a lot of time
at home. Sometimes I worked with the baby on my lap. My parents
also helped us out a few times a week.

I kept thinking about my mother, who had worked night shifts
at a factory and had still done all the cooking and cleaning and
child-rearing. How had she managed that? How had we all turned
out kind of OK? How had she not broken?

I decided not to breastfeed Sojourner because the few times I
tried, I could see a nervous breakdown coming in the distance.

The pressure to produce enough milk gave me anxiety. I figured that my daughter needed a functional mother more than she needed breast milk. I wasn't trying to be a hero to prove a point. I also didn't drink my placenta in a smoothie because I'm not a deviant or a Hollywood celebrity.

When Will and I were too tired to cook, we ordered food. Everything we needed, we simply bought. Diapers, formula, furniture, doodads, clothes, and whatever made caring for this baby easier. And boy was it expensive. I could not imagine caring for a newborn with the constraints of a full-time low-paying job. It shouldn't be that hard to take care of your baby just because you're working-class. The fact that the formula in our local stores was locked behind plastic is some classist bullshit that really gets me ranting. If you're in favor of babies going hungry, nine out of ten studies show that you're a complete asshole.

I'd be crying in the bathroom every day of my life if I worked more than forty hours a week in a factory and had to raise three children in an unfamiliar country with little to no help, the way my mom did. That requires extraordinary strength. A strength I'm not sure I possess.

Choosing how and when to have a family is critical to our liberation as women. Our society makes it nearly impossible for working mothers. And after having experienced the physical discomfort of pregnancy, I'm even more convinced that to force a woman to endure this against her will should be a crime. My abortion saved my life and made my current life possible. When I was depressed, I could barely get myself a glass of water, let alone help a child thrive. I wouldn't have been able to care for a baby in those circumstances. The reason that I was able to find joy in the movements inside my body was because I wanted this baby with every cell of my being. Because I willed her to exist, because I had been waiting for her for years and years. I can't imagine continuing a pregnancy that is not entirely my choice. It would be akin to torture. It makes me recoil to think that I almost had a baby with a dude who gave me phone accessories for Christmas.

SOMETIMES I IMAGINE what my relationship with Sojourner will be like in the future. I see us drinking coffee at an outdoor café in a picturesque foreign city, cackling at something, likely a man. We have many inside jokes and very long lunches. We go shopping. I rely on her to keep me from becoming frumpy and unfashionable. She tells me all the jargon the kids are saying. "Mija, what does it mean when the kids say, 'I bleep-blorped your mom'?"

Sometimes, though, I look at her and this is what happens in my brain: *What if you stop breathing? What if I drop you? What if I get postpartum depression and can't get out of bed? What if you don't want to go to college? What if someone calls you a racial slur? What if I fall down the stairs while I'm holding you? What if your spouse is intimidated by your greatness? What if you marry a white person? What if you get hit by a car? What if you get an incurable disease? What if someone hurts you? What if I hurt you? What if you become a vegan? At what point will you learn that your father and I are stoners? What if I say something well-intentioned but very stupid? What if you're so beautiful it becomes a danger? What if you inherit my shitty brain chemistry?*

And so on! And so forth! Et cetera and more. My mind is a hellscape. I'd like to take a vacation from myself most days. That's what my daily nap is all about. Like clockwork, I plummet hard in the afternoon because I have a difficult time being a person for an entire day. Instead of simply glowing in the magic that is my daughter, I mull over all the worst possible scenarios. I think of how I would never survive her absence from this world.

I'VE BEEN HAVING nightmares in which I have to move back to my childhood apartment, the place where I lived until I was eight years old. I remember the water stains on the walls, the cold showers that came out in weak trickles, the peeling brown linoleum in the kitchen, the Little Orphan Annie thrift store curtains, the violent fluorescent lighting, the drab and musty carpet in the living room whose original color was always a mystery. Once I snuck up to the attic of our building looking for anything of interest, but I only found wood beams and dust mites in the sunlight.

Why do I always return there in my dreams? What is it trying to tell me? What can't I let go of? My parents are still in Cicero, in the house we moved into when I was ten. Call it a suburb if you wish, but those of us from there know better. Cicero is a bleak place.

A lot of people I grew up with did stay in the area and I do not judge. It's hard to get out, and there's nothing wrong with staying there—whatever tickles your pickle—but from day one I was trying my best to get the fuck out of there. I would rather have died of a UTI than stay in the same place and work at a bank, married to a cop named Tony who pronounces the *l* in "salmon" and believes that blue lives matter.

Lately, I've been thinking about two of my childhood friends, who died when they were girls. I suppose I'm revisiting the dangers of girlhood now that I have a daughter. Motherhood has unearthed a lot of memories for me. My friends Vero and Sandra died in separate circumstances when I was in high school. Both of their deaths involved their boyfriends, but the rest is a mystery. I'll never know what actually happened. Vero left behind a baby who must be in his twenties by now. Sometimes I can see their bright young faces and wonder who they would've been today. It's taken me all these years to see that everyone—and I mean *everyone*—failed them.

LIVING WITH A mental illness is like walking a tightrope in heels: one misstep and you might plummet to your death. The wrong medication can ruin your entire life. Everything is high stakes. But now I know that some of my anxiety is inherited from my mother and all the women who came before us. My mother can always imagine the worst-case scenario because of all the terrible shit she's been through as a woman and as an immigrant. She's experienced traumas I'll likely never know about. Expecting the worst is simply a survival mechanism for her. It's taken me most of my life to realize that I, too, am always looking over my shoulder to see who or what might ruin my life.

I began to notice that I couldn't trust happiness a few years ago when I was in Italy on a research grant. It was 2018, just months after I had recovered from my most recent depressive episode. I was so happy to be there—fucking enchanted, really—but I couldn't take it in. I thought it was going to be taken away. It's as if I expected someone to come out of the shadows, slap the cannoli from my hand, and tell me I was bankrupt. Or I'd receive an email that said, "Lol, just kidding! Return your funds immediately." I just couldn't believe I could be there enjoying my life like that. Like, who do you think you are, some white bitch in a novel?

Similarly, many grown-up tasks give me an anxiety deep inside my butt. Doing taxes makes me faint. Simply filling out a W-2 gives me chorro. When buying our house, I had to produce endless documents, and it was so intrusive, I thought they'd eventually ask for the results of my latest pap smear. I was so distressed that I worried someone would discover I'd once filled out a form incorrectly and I would lose all my assets.

When you grow up Brown and poor, you feel like nothing belongs to you. You apologize for existing. You think white people are lurking in the bushes ready to ruin you, because they are!

It makes perfect sense that I was suicidal and that Latina teens have the highest suicide rate of their peer group. It's an epidemic that no one cares about because we hold such little value in this country. (A researcher named Dr. Luis Zayas has studied this extensively, and Soledad O'Brien and Maria Hinojosa have covered it as journalists.) Many young women living in traditional Latinx households feel as if they have no choices. For me, everyone had a say in what I did, how I dressed, how I acted, what my body looked like. It was as if my whole existence was an affront. Brown girls consider or commit suicide as a form of protest. You'd rather not exist than live in a way that tramples your spirit.

I understand some of my mother's anxiety, where it started and what it's become. There's only so much I can ever grasp. I know her childhood was devastatingly poor. Recently she shared that once she lost one of her shoes while playing in a stream and was left barefoot because they were her only pair. There's likely so much she will never say; she says she's forgotten most of it. Trauma is generational and sometimes we carry it without even knowing.

What we have in common is wanting more than our circumstances. When she decided to cross the border, she said *I will not live like this.* When I decided to leave home, I said the same. When I left my marriage. When I got an abortion.

Often the best choice is the hardest choice. Transformation is earned. It hurts. It's ugly. For so many years I held on to the guilt of not being the daughter my mother wanted, but now I see that we have done similar things. I have a deeper appreciation for her. I empathize with all she's been through, but I also understand that my mother's trauma is not for me to carry anymore. I'm not entirely sure what this means yet, but I do know that I refuse to pass it on. It ends with me.

When Sojourner was a few months old and I felt my body tense for no identifiable reason, I began to whisper out loud and in my head: "It's OK not to suffer." That has now transformed into "It's OK to be happy." When I say this, my muscles soften a bit, my shoulder blades relax, my jaw unclenches.

AFTER HAVING SOJOURNER we began to realize that our house felt cramped. It was a fine house, and if we'd needed to make it work we could have, but the issue for me was that I didn't have an office. It was starting to bum me out. I know how privileged that is, but I didn't work this hard to simply give up that dream. And to be frank, watching so much HGTV probably brainwashed me a bit. Also, I had an epiphany: we deserve nice things, too.

Will and I reviewed our finances and we started casually poking around. A few weeks in we found a stunning remodeled house in our neighborhood with a spiral staircase leading to a long, enormous attic. Will said it felt like a tree house and I agreed. I saw myself writing at the window, looking at the beautiful trees, my entire library behind me. It was some Virginia Woolf–type shit and I decided it was mine.

We immediately put in an offer, and we got it. After a very long and tedious process, we closed and moved in. Will and I were in disbelief that we were living in a house straight out of a sitcom. It still hasn't sunk in that we've been able to do this for our family. Every kid has their own room and Will and I both have offices.

I've decorated with what brings me joy: blue walls inspired by that village in Morocco I visited when I lived in Madrid, hummingbird wallpaper, prints by artists of color, colorful tapestries from different countries, my own art, a portrait of a Brown girl reading, Native American pottery, van Gogh wallpaper, Moroccan rugs, tarnished antiques, a portrait of Toni Morrison pontificating. It's bright and warm and unbelievably comfortable. It's a bit messy with books and art projects strewn about. I don't leave for days at a time.

A year after sheltering in place, we had a belated and vaccinated wedding in our new backyard with our closest friends and family. We wanted to celebrate in the place we love the most. We had a taquero and an all-woman mariachi. Paletas and churros for dessert and a taco piñata. Sojourner was the belle of the ball.

Our house is a place of creatures, big and small: three kids, a hateful cat, a dopey dog, and family and friends who stop by frequently. We have many casual gatherings of carefully curated people. Will and I have become even more vigilant about who we let into our lives. This is the safest I've ever felt. I tell people I plan to die here. This is the place I've been looking for my entire life.

I was almost convinced that I'd never be held and seen like this. My life is so idyllic that it almost gives me the willies. I have a cherubic Brown baby who laughs at everything I say. I'm married to a thicc king who loves it when I make art. We have roundtable discussions about race most nights. My career is exactly what I want it to be—I teach and write and travel. I take long walks in the park near my house, where I commune with flowers and trees. I have brilliant friends. My outfits are on point. I go where I please.

As I write this, many people are vaccinated in Chicago and it appears that we're slowly emerging from the pandemic. Of course I'm relieved that people will stop dying and that we can start breathing the same air, but in some ways, going back out into the world scares me. What crazy shit will white people say to me next? What if I forget how to act out there? Will and I are borderline feral. What if I go to a restaurant and order the chicken titty?

ALL I'VE EVER wanted was to feel alive. That is the thesis of my entire existence. I want to be terrified, astonished, furious, and delighted. I want to eat too much dinner and still order dessert. And coffee, because fuck it. I want to party so hard I lose a shoe. I want to laugh so much I actually pee my pants. I want to talk to a weirdo at a smelly dive bar. I want to cry in the street if the spirit moves me. I want to tell people how I feel even when it's uncomfortable. I want to make bad art that no one sees. I want to take a nap in a foreign country after a gigantic lunch. I want to fight and make up. I want to smoke weed with my husband in our yard. I want to be caught in a thunderstorm. I want to scream at a racist. I want to sleep too much. I want to paint trees with my daughter. I want to swim in the ocean at dusk. I want to cry until I pass out. I want to scare white people with my laughter. I want to write ridiculous poems with my stepkids. I want to stare out a window for as long as I like. I want to tell a stranger that she's beautiful. I want to fall in love with a cloud. I want to eat tacos at a flea market. I want to gasp at a painting. I want to crack a coconut. I want to write things that upset me. I want to cook a complicated meal. I want to wear flamboyant outfits. I want to weep over a book. I want to say I'm sorry. I want to say I forgive you. I want to sing poorly at my cat. I want to take my daughter to Paris on a whim. I want to be stunned by every sunset. I want to make beauty out of bullshit. I want to tell stories that are true.

Dear Sojourner,

    This is my life as best as I can remember it. I have fucked up in too many ways to name, but I have tried to challenge some of the wrongs of our past and present. I tried to make more space for you in this strange place called Earth. It's so hard to be human, to be female, to be alive. What I hope is that you will trust me with the truth, no matter how ugly, that you will let me hold your suffering when you need me to. I will never leave you.

Sojourner, the best fruit of my survival. You are of me, but you do not belong to me. What I want you to know is this: You are the most extraordinary creature. I am joy itself when I look at you. You come from women who refused to disappear. You are Brown and Black and glorious. You are boundless and magical and perfect. The world was not built for you, but there is beauty everywhere. My greatest wish is that you fight for it.

ACKNOWLEDGMENTS

Writing a book is never a solitary act. I have so many people to thank, both living and dead, for inspiring me to keep writing, to stay living.

Firstly, this book would not have been possible without my incredible editor, Georgia Bodnar. Georgia, you pushed me into so many uncomfortable places that I needed to see. Both my writing and thinking are sharper because of your eagle eye. Just so you know, I have plans on us being friends. It involves a lot of long lunches followed by coffee. Maybe some shopping or spa treatments. We'll see what happens. The kids are with the husbands.

Michelle Brower, you've been with me since the beginning of my publishing career. I vividly remember the time nobody wanted to take on my novel. You saw something no one else did, and I'm grateful for that. Thank you for always believing in the stories I tell. You've helped amplify my work in ways I couldn't even imagine. I hope we get to scarf down sushi in a crowded underground Midtown restaurant again soon, hunched over with coats in our laps while someone nearly elbows one of us in the face.

ACKNOWLEDGMENTS

Thank you to Emily Wunderlich for taking over this operation. I'm so happy I have your expertise as this thing becomes an actual book that people will read on toilets, trains, laps(?), and other interesting surfaces. Thanks in advance for your patience with me!

Thank you so much to the entire team at Viking. It's such an honor to work with you all. What a fucking dream. I'm grateful for all the attention and support you poured into this book.

Thank you, Princeton University and the Mellon Foundation, for the Princeton Arts Fellowship. I completed a great deal of this book during my time there.

To my best friend, Jen Fitzgerald. You are a real one. I wouldn't be here without you. I love you like a sister. I'm so happy I hitched that ride to Vermont that one time. I was never the same.

The following people and muppets have given me friendship and guidance for many years now; I'm eternally grateful for your presence in my life: Phillip B. Williams, Michael Harrington, Rigoberto González, Eduardo C. Corral, Safiya Sinclair, Maria Inés Zamudio, Sandra Cisneros, Miguel Jimenez, Jackson, Elizabeth Schmuhl, Sara Inés Calderón, Rachel Kahan, Anna Lekas Miller, Claudia Pineda, Xelena Gónzalez, and Julissa Arce.

Thank you, Ida Roldán, for your support during a difficult time.

I also must shout out Gary Dop, Christopher Gaumer, and the Randolph College Low Residency MFA program community. You're a beautiful team to work with.

The Latin American and Latino Studies Department at DePaul: thank you for supporting my writing and teaching. Can we please have a happy hour now? This is getting ridiculous.

ACKNOWLEDGMENTS

My brothers: you are the worst, but also the best. Let us celebrate this book with wet meat sandwiches.

Sof, Teo, and Nora—your creativity inspires me. Thanks for always being my buds.

None of this would have been possible without my parents, Catarina and Gustavo Sánchez.

Bean and Spike, you were an unexpected and delightful addition to my life. I think Professor Sausage would be very proud of you two right now.

To my beloved husband, "Will": I didn't know that a man like you could exist in this world. Thank you for always happily supporting my work and providing endless laughter and inspiration. I love you so much it's gross. Meet me in the attic for a roundtable discussion on the true meaning of the word "nutrient."

Sojourner Inés, I'm so excited to see the woman you will become. You are magical. You are perfect.

SOURCES

Down to Clown

Frank Rich. "In Conversation with Chris Rock." *Vulture.* https://www.vulture.com/2014/11/chris-rock-frank-rich-in-conversation.html.

Peter McGraw and Joel Warner. *The Humor Code: A Global Search for What Makes Things Funny.* New York: Simon & Schuster, 2014.

Olga Khazan. "Plight of the Funny Female." *Atlantic,* November 19, 2015. https://www.theatlantic.com/health/archive/2015/11/plight-of-the-funny-female/416559/.

"Make Her Laugh." *Science,* vol. 311, no. 5761. February 3, 2006, p. 587.

Christopher Hitchens. "Why Women Still Don't Get It." *Vanity Fair,* April 2008. https://www.vanityfair.com/culture/2008/04/hitchens200804.

"Comedians Have 'High Levels of Psychotic Traits.'" BBC News, January 16, 2014. https://www.bbc.com/news/health-25747068.

Back to the Motherland

Charlotte M. Gradie. *The Tepehuan Revolt of 1616: Militarism, Evangelism, and Colonialism in Seventeenth-Century Nueva Vizcaya.* Salt Lake City: University of Utah Press, 2000.

Rebecca Solnit. *A Field Guide to Getting Lost.* New York: Penguin, 2005.

Virginia Woolf and Mary Gordon. *A Room of One's Own.* Boston: Harcourt, 2005.

La Mala Vida

Rebecca Solnit. *The Faraway Nearby.* New York: Penguin, 2014.

Jean-Paul Sartre, Richard Howard, and James Wood. *Nausea.* New York: New Directions, 2013.

Nick Flynn. *Some Ether.* Minneapolis: Graywolf Press, 2000.

Christopher Hitchens. "Mommie Dearest." *Slate*, October 20, 2003. https:// slate.com/news-and-politics/2003/10/the-fanatic-fraudulent-mother-teresa .html.

Rebecca Solnit. *Hope in the Dark: Untold Histories, Wild Possibilities.* Chicago: Haymarket Books, 2016.

Soka Gakkai. https://www.sgi.org/about-us/buddhist-concepts/changing-poison -into-medicine.html.

Woody Hochswender, Greg Martin, and Ted Morino. *The Buddha in Your Mirror: Practical Buddhism and the Search for Self.* Middleway Press, 2001.

Pema Chödrön. *When Things Fall Apart: Heart Advice for Difficult Times.* Boulder, CO: Shambhala, 2016.

Ntozake Shange. *For Colored Girls Who Have Considered Suicide/When the Rainbow Is Enuf: A Choreopoem.* New York: Scribner, 2010.

Do You Think I'm Pretty? Circle Yes or No

John Charles Chasteen. *Born in Blood and Fire: A Concise History of Latin America.* New York: W. W. Norton, 2016.

Naomi Wolf. *The Beauty Myth: How Images of Beauty Are Used Against Women.* New York: HarperCollins, 2011.

Elaine Scarry. *On Beauty and Being Just.* Princeton, NJ: Princeton University Press, 2010.

Nicholas Mirzoeff. *An Introduction to Visual Culture.* Oxfordshire, UK: Routledge, 2009.

I Like to Enjoy

Octavio Paz. *The Labyrinth of Solitude and The Other Mexico; Return to the Labyrinth of Solitude; Mexico and the United States; The Philanthropic Ogre.* New York: Grove Press, 2001.

Virginia Woolf and Mary Gordon. *A Room of One's Own.* Boston: Harcourt, 2005.

Naomi Wolf. *Vagina: A New Biography.* London, UK: Virago, 2013.

Difficult Sun

Kay Jamison. *Touched with Fire.* New York: Free Press, 1994.